Children's Traditional Games

Children's Traditional Games

Games from 137 Countries and Cultures

by
Judy Sierra
Robert Kaminski

Oryx Press
1995

The rare Arabian Oryx is believed to have inspired the myth of the unicorn. This desert antelope became virtually extinct in the early 1960s. At that time several groups of international conservationists arranged to have 9 animals sent to the Phoenix Zoo to be the nucleus of a captive breeding herd. Today the Oryx population is over 1000, and over 500 have been returned to the Middle East.

© 1995 by Judy Sierra and Robert Kaminski
Published by The Oryx Press
4041 North Central at Indian School Road
Phoenix, Arizona 85012-3397

Published simultaneously in Canada

Printed and Bound in the United States of America

∞ The paper used in this publication meets the minimum requirements of American National Standard for Information Science—Permanence of Paper for Printed Library Materials, ANSI Z39.48, 1984.

Library of Congress Cataloging-in-Publication Data

Sierra, Judy.
  Children's traditional games : games from 137 countries and cultures / by Judy Sierra, Robert Kaminski.
      p. cm.
  Includes bibliographical references and index.
  ISBN 0-89774-967-7 (pbk. : alk. paper)
    1. Games—Cross-cultural studies.   2. Games—Study and teaching (Elementary) 3. Children and folklore.   I. Kaminski, Robert.
  II. Title.
GR480.S54   1995
796'.545—dc20   95-35623
                                                                 CIP

Contents

Contents

Contents

Preface

This book was written to fill an important reference need and to promote a great teaching idea. A collection of traditional games played by children in as many of the world's countries and cultures as possible has long been needed. The idea of compiling such a work was suggested to us by the editors of the Oryx Press, and a survey of our local school and public librarians quickly confirmed the demand for it.

According to these librarians, there are two audiences for this book: teachers and group leaders looking for games for children to play in the classroom and at multicultural festivals; and students seeking cultural material such as games to include in assigned reports on countries. There was neither an index to games nor an anthology of games available that had anything approaching a systematic, worldwide treatment.

The great teaching idea promoted in this book is using children's traditional games as a focus of multicultural studies in the elementary grades. These games are ideal for the study of cultural traditions since a) they exist in every ethnic group, neighborhood, and family, not just among a few cultures, and b) they form a part of the living folklife of children, who understand them intuitively. This book provides a rationale for such studies and step-by-step lesson plans in which students compare and contrast games and collect games from family, friends, and community members.

SCOPE

We have included in this book games from as many of the world's nations and cultures as possible. In cases where a particular game was played in several countries, we included the game under one country with cross-references to it in the index. When no game at all is given for a particular country, either in Chapter 3, "Games Treasury," or the index, this means that we were not able to locate one (or at least one that met the criteria for this collection). This book includes 204 games from 137 countries and cultures.

The games in this book are traditional children's games, which we define as those that are played informally with minimal equipment, that children learn by example from other children, and that can be played without reference to written rules. These games are usually played by children between the ages of 7 and 12, with some latitude on both ends of the age range. Generally, children younger than 7 have difficulty remembering and following game rules and play only alongside older players; quite a bit of physical, mental, and social skill is required by nearly all traditional children's games. In most industrial societies, children stop playing traditional childhood games around the age of 12. Some of the games in the book—mainly board games, but also athletic competitions such as ball games—are also played by adults; this is noted in each case. As played by adults, these games can be quite complex; children generally play them with less skill and strategy.

CRITERIA FOR INCLUSION

Games are included in this book on the basis of appropriateness for classroom, library, and recreational settings. We made these decisions based on our experience as former game players and teachers. Approximately one-third of the games were tested in elementary classrooms by Bob Kaminski as part of his work as a substitute teacher in Ashland and Eugene, Oregon, in the 1993–1994 and 1994–1995 school years.

We chose to include games that we thought could be played with a minimum of preparations and that older elementary children could recreate themselves without adult assistance. We excluded games we considered dangerous, such as the North American game of Mumblety-Peg, which involves throwing knives, and widely distributed "horse" games in which one or several children jump on another's back. Other types of games, such as complicated handclapping or singing games, were omitted because they are difficult to recreate solely on the basis of descriptions and drawings.

Finally, we have tried to achieve a balance of game types across the collection so that a teacher wishing to study, for example, several types of hopscotch will find a selection from widely different geographic areas.

ORGANIZATION

The book is organized into three parts, along with a bibliography and an index.

Part 1, "Games and Culture," provides an introduction to children's traditional games. In Chapter 1, "Children and Games," we define traditional children's games, contrast them with other kinds of games, and present an overview of academic research on the subject. In Chapter 2, "Types of Traditional Games," we describe specific types or categories of traditional games. There is no single accepted classification scheme for these games. In this chapter, we have classified the games into fairly standard game types, using category names that are readily understood by children, such as ball games and tag. We discuss the distinguishing features of each game type across cultures. A list is provided of all the games in each category found in Chapter 3, "Games Treasury," as well as, for some game types, a bibliography of books and articles for further reading.

Part 2, "The Games," describes a selection of traditional games. In Chapter 3, "Games Treasury," 204 children's games from 137 countries and cultures are explained. The number of players, playing area, and materials required for play are listed at the beginning of each game for ease in locating games for specific groups, environments, and situations.

For the sake of authenticity, the games in the "Games Treasury" are presented as we found them; that is, we have not invented missing rules or converted narrative descriptions of the games into step-by-step instructions. We have, however, rewritten the descriptions for clarity and combined material from various sources to give the most complete account of each game. In many instances we suggest easily acquired substitutes for the traditional materials used to play the games.

We have included the native-language name of each game as well as other native-language terms given in our sources, though we have not attempted to translate them unless the author of the source did so. Experience with the archaic and specialized vocabularies of English-language traditional games and rhymes led us to understand that many of the words used in games do not carry the literal dictionary meanings. Translation of material such as this is a tricky business best left to language experts.

Part 3, "Games and Teaching," provides ideas and lesson plans for using children's traditional games in the classroom and library. In Chapter 4, "Collecting and Exploring Traditional Games," we encourage the collecting of games from family, friends, and relatives. This section ends with a description of a week-long, multicultural games festival held at Nimitz Elementary School in Cupertino, California, in 1992.

The Bibliography begins with the authors' recommendations of the best sources of additional games. The remainder of the bibliography includes all of the authors' sources for the book, subdivided geographically. Two indexes complete the book. One, "Index to Playing Environments," provides readers with a listing of the games arranged by the playing surface or location most appropriate for a game, such as "pavement," or "classroom or living room." The "General Index" provides an index to all other names and subjects in this book.

RESEARCH METHODOLOGY

Because we were familiar with the literature of the field when we began work on this project, we understood very well why no comparable work existed. The primary source materials are scattered across a wide variety of disciplines, are not well indexed, and are in a variety of languages. Judy Sierra brought to this task a knowledge of resources in academic folklore and anthropology and a reading knowledge of French, German, and Spanish. Most of the research for this book was done in the libraries of the University of California, Los Angeles and Berkeley campuses, and the University of Oregon. While sitting amongst the library stacks seaching the indexes of individual works of folklore and anthropology, we met several elementary school students and their parents who were desperately trying to satisfy teachers' demands for games from a specific country; this reinforced our conviction that this book is sorely needed.

Through our work with immigrant children in California, we had much firsthand knowledge of children's games from 20 or so countries. However, because of the historical depth and geographical scope envisioned for this work, we decided to include only games that were documented in reliable printed sources. We hope to compile a companion volume to the present one that will include games from as many cultures as possible, collected from people who actually played them. Those with games to share are invited to submit a description of the game to the authors, along with information about when and where the game was played.

ACKNOWLEGMENTS

We would like to thank the staff of the Oryx Press, and especially Art Stickney, for their encouragement in what often seemed an impossible task, and the interlibrary loan staff of Jackson County Library in Medford, Oregon, for bringing us old and rare books from around the country. We are especially grateful to the parents, students, and staffs of Rosemont Elementary School in Los Angeles and of Nimitz Elementary School in Cupertino, California, who taught us their traditional games and played them with us.

PART I
Games and Culture

Chapter 1
Children and Games

People in every part of the world pursue activities that do not seem essential to their survival. In industrialized societies, play activities are often considered trivial and defined as the opposite of work. Work is valued, while play is not.

However, most social scientists agree that play is not only a normal part of human life, it is an essential part. Play is necessary for children's healthy development, helping them acquire physical, social, and cognitive skills. For adults, play provides a release from the pressures and stresses of everyday life.

Games are a specialized form of play: they proceed according to predetermined patterns or rules, and have predictable outcomes. Children's traditional games (also called folk games) are those that are passed from child to child, generation to generation, informally by word of mouth. They come in a variety of forms and types. Most games of physical skill, strategy, and chance are competitive. However, many children's traditional games are fundamentally cooperative, such as dramatic and singing games, and hand-clapping games, in which the players' goal is to complete a pattern or patterns. Most children's traditional games include two or more of the following six components, in varying degrees depending on the game:

- Physical skill

- Strategy

- Chance

- Repetition of patterns

- Creativity

- Vertigo

(The last component, vertigo, was identified by the French scholar and poet Roger Caillois and will be easily understood by anyone who has played Ring around the Rosie, London Bridge, or tag. Vertigo is the wild release of collapsing in a heap after a tug of war, or the thrill of running in mock fear from "It.")

The following are a few examples of the way the components of children's traditional games coexist in a single game. In London Bridge, a short ritual song or drama (repetition of patterns) precedes each player choosing one of two words to determine teams (chance), and that in turn precedes a tug-of-war (physical skill), which ends in collapse (vertigo). Counting out combines traditional rhymes (repetition of patterns) with chance; counting out precedes games of physical skill and strategy, such as tag or hide-and-seek, to determine who will be in the special position of the game, such as "It." Creativity is particularly encouraged in certain types of traditional games, such as dramatic and pantomime games, and storytelling and word games. It is also exhibited in individuals' playing styles.

As children's activities, traditional games differ from both adult-organized sports and manufactured or educational games (even though many modern athletic competitions originated as folk games and manufacturers often package and sell folk games). The following are some of the characteristics of traditional games and of children's traditional games in particular:

- Children organize traditional games for their own pleasure. Children themselves are the experts, and they decide when, where, and how to play.

- Traditional games have rules, but the rules are not written down (or need not be written down). The rules are easy for players to remember. A group of children can recall them well enough to agree upon them and abide by them.

- The rules of traditional games are negotiable. The basic rules and play-patterns are so finely tuned to children's abilities and interests that tampering with them (especially by well-meaning adults) may ruin the game. However, dozens of minor, player-created variations do exist. Rules are often negotiated before or during play, especially if the players are not accustomed to playing together.

- Children usually learn to play traditional games by standing on the sidelines and watching other children play, not by receiving instruction. Sometimes younger children and children who have not yet been accepted as players practice alone.

- Traditional games are simple enough to be played by a child of normal abilities who is motivated to learn. Most folk games also offer opportunities for players to achieve advanced competency in strategy or physical skill. Players may not be aware of or able to explain the strategies they use.

- Traditional games are both competitive and cooperative, though one aspect or the other usually predominates. They are cooperative because they cannot continue unless all players agree to continue playing and to play by the rules. Many traditional games lack any provision for determining a winner. Games that could have a winner, such as hopscotch, are often abandoned by the players before a winner is determined, especially if players must wait too long for their turns. Punishments for the losers of a game, in the form of taunts, blows, forfeits, and penalties, are more common in children's traditional games than are rewards for winners.

- Folk games do not require manufactured equipment; they can be played with found or homemade objects. For example, the board game *Seega* is played on a wooden board inlaid with ivory, with metal game pieces. It is also played on diagrams marked in the dirt, with seeds or stones as game pieces. Because we now live in an environment filled with manufactured items, it is not surprising that traditional games have evolved using recycled or even purchased materials. The game of POG, for instance, was invented by kids in Hawaii. They played with milk caps from a local dairy and got the name of the game from a fruit juice the dairy manufactured made of *p*assionfruit, *o*ranges, and *g*uavas. The current POG craze began in 1991 when an elementary school teacher taught the game, which she remembered from her childhood, to her students. Within a few years, the game spread across North American, and it was being played with manufactured discs that never touched a milk bottle. In many cases, manufactured objects make traditional games easier to play. Six-pointed metal or plastic jacks are much easier to pick up than the animal bones or pebbles they replaced; a rubber ball that can be tossed up in the air and caught after one bounce gives a player more time to pick up the jacks than a pebble that must be caught before it hits the ground.

THE GAMES ARE ANCIENT, THE PLEASURE IS NEW

A fascinating aspect of children's traditional games is the extent to which they have remained unchanged over the years. Today, children in Mediterranean countries play games such as Blind Man's Bluff, knucklebones, and *Morra* in very much the same way these games were played in Ancient Egypt, Greece, and Rome. The words of songs and chants that accompany many European folk games appear to have changed little since the Middle Ages. Scholars have shown that some of these words relate to beliefs and customs that were abandoned by adults long ago.

While it is true that the remnants of religious and seasonal rituals can be found in today's children's games, this does not mean that, over the centuries, children have repeated games like robots. Traditional games fill a need in children's lives and have survived because they provide a reliable framework for enjoyable play, as well as opportunities for creativity and exploration.

WORLDWIDE SIMILARITIES AMONG GAMES

Not only do children's traditional games tend to maintain the same form and even the same words over hundreds or thousands of years, the same types of games—hide-and-seek, blind man's bluff, hopscotch, and jacks, just to name a few—are found in widely separated and fundamentally different cultures. The question of how games came to be so widespread has never been answered. In most cases, researchers lack physical or written evidence to draw reliable conclusions. Where evidence does exist, answers to questions of games' origin and diffusion can be proposed. For example, we know that *Alquerque* was a very popular board game in Spain at the time of the Spanish conquest of the Americas. Alquerque-type games played by Native Americans, such as the Zuni *Kolowis Awithlaknannai* and the Tarascan *El Coyote,* were probably originally learned from the Spanish. There is no archaeological evidence for these games before the conquest, though there is preconquest evidence for other Native American board games, such as the Aztec *Patolli.* Researchers can only speculate whether the worldwide occurrence of games such as jacks or hopscotch is due to natural human inclinations to engage in certain activities, or to the spread of a game through conquest, migration, or trade.

When one looks at a type of game across cultures, the similarities are usually more striking than the differences, which suggests that games are typical human activities rather than typical of the culture in which they are played. Judith Van Hoorn studied the games mothers and babies play among four ethnic groups in San Joaquin County, California. Hispanic, Filipino, Chinese, and Anglo mothers and babies were observed. Mothers of the first three groups did not use English in their baby games, even if they spoke English well. Van Hoorn concluded:

> In contrast to what I had expected, I found striking similarities among the games from the four cultures. . . . There was little difference in the way that mothers played the games and the actions of the games. The main difference was the language used and what was said. . . . Rather than enculturating infants . . . infant games help foster a more universal process, that is, they "enspeciate."

The same could be said of most traditional children's games. They are human activities first, culture-specific activities second.

TRADITIONAL GAMES AND CULTURAL DIFFERENCES

Teachers are interested in the ways games relate to culture. Folklorist Brian Sutton-Smith summarized what anthropological studies have revealed about this question:

- Traditional games reward behaviors that have cultural value.

- More complex cultures have more complex games and more types of games.

- Agricultural and industrial societies have more games of strategy; nomadic societies, in which life is more uncertain, have more games of chance.

Among games from the same culture, some game rules mirror the rules of everyday life. In this way, they can be said to prepare children for adult life. The South African game *Dithwai* helps children develop visual memory skill needed for tending cattle, for example. Other games from the same culture mock and overturn the rules of everyday life. In this way, they can be said to relieve the stress caused by these rules, and even suggest ways these rules could or should be changed. Games of forfeits can be seen as commentaries on the seemingly arbitrary nature of adults' punishments of children.

The study of games and how they relate to the whole of a culture requires in-depth knowledge of both the culture and comparable games from other cultures. At the upper-elementary or high school level, study of the relationship of folk games to culture may begin with an examination of the games in students' own cultures. Suggestions for projects that lead students toward their own insights and conclusions about folk games are presented in Chapter 4: "Collecting and Exploring Traditional Games."

GAMES AND CHILD DEVELOPMENT

The types of traditional games in this book are played by children roughly between the ages of seven and 12. Although younger children play alone and in groups, the ability to skillfully play a game with predetermined rules or patterns seems to be attained at about the same age that a child has the maturity to function in a structured classroom. (Seven is also the age at which children in traditional agricultural and hunting societies begin to take on responsibilities that contribute to the survival of the community.)

Children become interested spectators of the folk games of older children at around the age of four. Herbert and Mary Knapp documented the inclusion and exclusion of younger brothers and sisters in children's traditional games. The younger children and their parents often insisted on inclusion, despite the objections of the older children. Younger children's lack of skill was better accommodated in games, such as tag and hide-and-seek, where their presence did not greatly affect the outcome or other players' enjoyment. Older children sometimes taught strategy to the younger ones; at other times they sought to free themselves of their younger siblings as quickly as possible. A few traditional games are tailor-made for mixed-age groups though, such as the Are You Ready? games (see page 35) and the line tag games (see page 35).

Most folk games keep a child's interest for a year, or two or three at most, and so players advance quickly from beginner to expert level. Children stop playing a particular game when it no longer provides a challenge. For example, most children cease playing Tic Tac Toe soon after they learn that the player who goes first, if she uses correct strategy, cannot lose. They also stop playing particular games because of changes in the weather or in their schedules or because of peer pressure to do so.

The Knapps developed a theory that children's games are a laboratory of social relationships. and that as such, they are extremely important to healthy development. Games do not simply teach children preexisting values and rules. They allow children to test the limits of acceptable behavior, and they provide a framework within which children learn, firsthand and without adult intervention, how to get along together.

Like all unsupervised children's activities, traditional games provide opportunities for ostracism and cruelty. These aspects can be minimalized when games are used in the classroom. Traditional games offer a variety of roles that allow children to take turns trying on the personas of villain, hero, and heroine. Fairness and inclusion are a potential in folk games that is realized over time, but may not be readily apparent to an adult observing only one play session. Many folk games encourage healthy exercise, without the pressures of winning and losing or the exclusion of poor players. A child is more likely to be excluded from a traditional game for poor attitude than for inferior athletic abilities. Another healthy aspect of traditional games is that the individual players are continually starting over from scratch; there is no season record hanging over their heads. Also, the players of folk games plan their own strategies, a role that is usually taken over by adult coaches in organized children's sports.

The theory that children's games provide essential training in social interaction has very important implications. At a time when much of children's play is dictated by video and computer games—games in which the major social interaction skill taught is pulling a trigger—it is very important for adults to encourage the playing of traditional children's games. The example of the teacher who sparked the POG revival shows that adults can do this successfully.

BOYS' GAMES, GIRLS' GAMES

In most cultures, some folk games are considered boys' games, others are considered girls' games, and still others are played by mixed groups. However, the same game may be a girls' game in one culture and a boys' or mixed group game in another. For example, hopscotch, which is generally considered a girls' game in the United States, is played chiefly by boys in some cultures, such as the native Tarascan and Zapotec of Mexico. Rope skipping, now thought of as a girls' game in the United States, was eagerly played by both boys and girls a hundred years ago. The Knapps observed that, in general, "girls' games" require that players master certain predetermined patterns of words and motions, while "boys' games" demand that players change strategy (improvise) as the game progresses. The Knapps contended that boys do not play girls' games, while girls are eager to join in boys' games.

These conclusions are contradicted by our own experience and observations that both boys and girls want and need both types of challenges. According to Fred Ferretti, author of *The Great American Book of Sidewalk, Stoop, Dirt, Curb, and Alley Games:*

> Just as boys chauvinistically expect girls to stay away from the roughhousing that they regarded as their special province, girls regard jump rope as an activity that boys really aren't interested in. And just as surely as the boys' assumption is not totally true, neither is the girls'. I can remember playing jump rope, enjoying it immensely, and coming back for more.

In a study of children's games played in a Thai village in the 1970s, Wanni Wibalswadi Anderson discovered that exclusively girls' games and exclusively boys' games were played much more frequently at school than in the home neighborhood. Boys and girls played together more at home, and played games that their genders would preclude at school. It seems likely that children at school have a strong tendency to play gender-specific games (much of the Knapps' research was conducted on school playgrounds), and that adult expectations and peer pressure influence game choice far more than natural desires or abilities.

Whatever the cause of gender differences in folk games, adults who work with children cannot ignore their existence. Teachers need to be familiar with their students' attitudes toward game participation by gender so that they do not unintentionally subject children to teasing or ridicule. This does not mean that gender preference in games can not be a subject of class discussion. And this type of gender separation does not exist at all schools. In the fifth grade, our son played jacks and jump rope with both boys and girls.

Teachers and parents can encourage the playing of traditional folk games by respecting, encouraging, and celebrating them, and by enforcing each child's right to a safe neighborhood in which to play.

Recommended Reading

Anderson, Wanni Wibalswadi. "Ecological and Sociocultural Determinants in Thai Children's Game-Playing Event." In *The Paradoxes of Play,* ed. John Loy, pp. 167–75. West Point, N.Y.: Leisure Press, 1982.

Caillois, Roger. *Man, Play and Games.* New York: Free Press of Glencoe, 1961.

Ferretti, Fred. *The Great American Book of Sidewalk, Stoop, Dirt, Curb, and Alley Games.* New York: Workman, 1975.

Knapp, Herbert, and Knapp, Mary. *One Potato, Two Potato: The Secret Education of American Children.* New York: W.W. Norton, 1976.

Monighan-Nourot, Patricia, et al., eds. *Looking at Children's Play: A Bridge between Theory and Practice.* New York: Teachers College Press, 1987.

Mouledoux, Elizabeth D. "The Development of Play in Childhood: An Application of the Classifications of Piaget and Caillois in Developmental Research." In *Studies in the Anthropology of Play,* ed. Phillips Stevens, Jr., pp. 196–207. West Point, N.Y.: Leisure Press, 1977.

Stevens, Phillips Jr. "Laying the Groundwork for an Anthropology of Play." In *Studies in the Anthropology of Play,* ed. Phillips Stevens, Jr., pp. 237–249. West Point, N.Y.: Leisure Press, 1977.

Sutton-Smith, Brian. "Towards an Anthropology of Play." In *Studies in the Anthropology of Play,* ed. Phillips Stevens, Jr., pp. 222–232. West Point, N.Y.: Leisure Press, 1977.

Van Hoorn, Judith. "Games That Babies and Mothers Play." In *Looking at Children's Play: A Bridge between Theory and Practice*, ed. Patricia Monighan-Nourot, et al. New York: Teachers College Press, 1987.

Chapter 2
Types of Traditional Games

Traditional games fall naturally into categories or types of games, based on patterns of play and the objects used to play them. However, there is no standard classification system for traditional games, so we have created our own, using terms that we think our readers will naturally use, such as jacks, hopscotch, tag, and marbles. As a glance through the following pages will quickly reveal, similar games are played in widely different geographical and cultural areas.

The following categories include most, though not all, of the games in this book. Some games just do not seem to belong to larger categories, even if they are played in more than one area. Also, traditional games are complex, and some fall into more than one category. For example, in the game Lemonade (page 156), an original pantomime by one team turns into a game of tag the moment one player on the other team guesses what is being mimed. We have included a reference to this game in two categories, drama and pantomime games, and tag.

BALL GAMES

Balls have been used in sports, games, and pastimes throughout history and in all parts of the world. An Ancient Egyptian mural from a tomb at Beni Hasan shows a group of women throwing balls back and forth. When Columbus landed on the island of Hispaniola, he found the inhabitants playing games with balls made of rubber. Rubber was at that time unknown in Europe, though the people of Central and South America had been making both solid and hollow rubber balls for at least 500 years. People who did not live in rubber-producing areas made balls from sewn and stuffed animal hides, inflated animal bladders, and fibers wound like balls of yarn. Native Americans in the southwestern United States have for centuries made foot-racing balls by carving and shaping yucca root, mesquite wood, or light volcanic rock into spheres and coating them with sticky mesquite gum or creosote. In Southeast Asia, hollow balls are woven of rattan. The native Yághan of Tierra del Fuego, at the southernmost tip of South America, played with balls made by stuffing seal bladders with feathers. Obviously, these nonrubber balls were made for tossing in the air or kicking along the ground, rather than bouncing. Solid, high-bouncing rubber balls were made only after the invention of the vulcanization process in the nineteenth century.

In traditional games, balls are kicked along the ground during foot races, kicked in the air repeatedly to see how long they can be kept aloft, juggled, hit with bats, rolled at targets, and thrown at players in tag games. Many traditional games, especially those in which a ball is thrown, are not played with balls that are hard or perfectly round. In re-creating these games with children, consider using beanbags or other soft or stuffed balls instead of hard rubber or plastic balls.

See the following ball games in the Games Treasury:

ARGENTINA (NATIVE ARAUCANIANS): *PILLMA*

BANGLADESH: *GUL TARA* (TOSSING TO THE STARS)

GUATEMALA: WALL BOUNCE

LUXEMBOURG: HOOP GAME

NEW ZEALAND: FOLDING ARMS

UNITED KINGDOM (ENGLAND): MONDAY, TUESDAY

UNITED STATES: A, MY NAME IS ALICE

UNITED STATES (NATIVE AMERICAN—WINNEBAGO): *HAHI'BIDJIKEEUN* (TREE GAME)

BLINDFOLD GAMES

In most blindfold games, one player, selected to be It, is blindfolded and then spun around several times. It then tries to catch one of the other players. In some games, It must identify, by touching him or by the sound of his voice, the player caught. The playing space used for blindfold games must be fairly small, otherwise It does not stand a chance of catching anyone. However, the strategy of players in blindfold games is not merely to try to avoid capture. They tease It, trying to get very close and even touch It without being tagged. When It succeeds in catching someone, that player becomes It.

Blindfold games are played in nearly every part of the world. In England and the United States, the game is usually called Blind Man's Bluff. The game is also called Blind Hob and Blind Bucky Davy in England, *Kattamougia* in Cyprus, *Klappe Hynde* in Denmark, *Pime Sikk* in Estonia, *Kauransyöttö* in Finland, *Blinde Kuh* in Germany, *Po-ai-pu-ni* in Hawaii, *Dumpwie* in Liberia, *Laumineti* in Lithuania, *Korosora* in New Guinea, *Boju-boju* in Nigeria, *Takip-silem* in the Philippines, *La Gallina Ciega* in Spain and Latin America, *Spänna* or *Spåna Kyrka* in Sweden, *Zmirkanje* in Yugoslavia, and *Ing'ombe Ingota* in Zimbabwe. It is also played in China, Japan, the Netherlands, Turkey, and Iran, and by many Native American groups, from the Inuit of Alaska to the Yághans of Tierra del Fuego.

See the following blindfold games in the Games Treasury:

CHINA: CALLING THE CHICKENS

EL SALVADOR: *LA GALLINA CIEGA* (THE BLIND HEN)

FINLAND: *STEAK*

FRANCE: *LES GRELOTS* (BELL TAG)

GREECE (ANCIENT): BRAZEN FLY

YEMEN: NAME TAG

Two-Person Blindfold Games

In another type of blindfold game, only two people play at a time. Each one holds onto one end of a rope, and the middle of the rope is tied to a tree or a post. One player is blindfolded and tries to tag the other, who must always respond when her name is called.

See the following two-person blindfold game in the Games Treasury:

CROATIA: JACK, WHERE ARE YOU?

BOARD GAMES

Before the invention of paper or plastic, diagrams for games of strategy were scratched in sand or clay, or carved in wood or stone. In Ancient Egypt, pharaohs played the game of Senet on boards made of wood and ivory, while peasants played the same game on diagrams scratched in the dirt. Some of the oldest board games known are the morris games (see United Kingdom [England]: Three Men's Morris for an example). Morris diagrams have been found at a Bronze Age burial site in Ireland, at the first city of Troy, carved into the steps of a first century A.D. shrine in Sri Lanka, and on a roof tile of the Ancient Egyptian Temple at Kurna, which was built in about 1400 B.C. Today we play a game like Three Men's Morris called Tic Tac Toe. Morris game markers may be beans, shells, or seeds, or exquisitely carved ivory or cast metal pieces.

The board games included in this book are not necessarily as simple as they seem. We have chosen to include traditional board-type games that children can *begin* to play without memorizing complex rules and strategies. The strategies used by experienced players of these same games is quite complex, especially in the case of the African mancala games, such as *Awele* from the Ivory Coast.

See the following board games in the Games Treasury:

CHINA: *SZ'KWA*

EGYPT: *SEEGA*

GHANA: *ACHI*

ICELAND: FOX AND GEESE

INDIA: VULTURES AND CROWS

IVORY COAST: *AWELE*

MEXICO (NATIVE TARASCAN): *EL COYOTE*

SPAIN: *ALQUERQUE*

SRI LANKA: COWS AND LEOPARDS

SUDAN: *DALA*

UNITED KINGDOM (ENGLAND): THREE MEN'S MORRIS

UNITED STATES (NATIVE AMERICAN—PIMA): *GINS* (STICKS)

UNITED STATES (NATIVE AMERICAN—ZUNI): *KOLOWIS AWITHLAKNANNAI* (FIGHTING SERPENTS)

Further Reading

Bell, Robert Charles. *Board and Table Games from Many Civilizations.* 2nd ed. London: Oxford University Press, 1969.

Bell, Robbie, and Cornelius, Michael. *Board Games 'Round the World: A Resource Book for Mathematical Investigations.* New York: Cambridge University Press, 1988.

Botermans, Jack, et al., eds. *World of Games: Their Origins and History, How to Play Them and How to Make Them.* New York: Facts on File, 1987.

Murray, Harold James Ruthven. *A History of Board Games Other than Chess.* Oxford: Claredon, 1952.

CATEGORY GAMES

Some traditional games require that players name things that belong to certain categories. In one type of category game, a leader names various animals, then the other players must immediately make a sign to indicate whether that animal has horns (in one game) or flies (in another). In other category games, players must take turns naming items in a certain category until the category is exhausted, or they must name items in a category that begin with a certain letter of the alphabet.

See the following category games in the Games Treasury:

GERMANY: *ALLE VÖGEL VLIEGEN* (ALL BIRDS FLY)

LATVIA: HORNS, HORNS, WHO HAS HORNS?

SWITZERLAND: *HALLIHALLO*

UNITED STATES: CATEGORIES

UNITED STATES: CATEGORIES HOPSCOTCH

COUNTING OUT

The ways game players choose sides or decide who will play first or who will take the role of It are often small games in themselves. Deciding who or which team will play first may be accomplished by the toss of a coin, by drawing straws, or by going hand over hand up a stick or bat. Depending upon the game, the role of It is either sought after or avoided. In some games, It is a leadership role that many players want, and the first player to shout for it gets the job. In other games, It is an undesirable role; in hide-and-seek, for instance, It has to work hard and everyone is against It. When choosing It for these games, players may shout "Not It," leaving an inattentive player to take the role. Japanese children count out using *Jan Ken Po,* a game like Scissors-Paper-Stone.

Counting-out rhymes are used to eliminate candidates for the job of It one by one. Folklorist Kenneth Goldstein discovered that crafty players often control the outcome of such choosing routines as "Eeny, meeny, miny, mo" and "One potato, two potato." These players take the role of the "counter" and are always able to control the choice of It by manipulating the number of beats they give to the rhyme or by knowing where to begin the count so that it ends where they want it to.

Folk rhymes have long been used for counting out in countries around the world. Many of the words in these rhymes no longer make sense (perhaps some never did). These nonsense words give the rhyme the mystique of a magic formula. Some traditional English language counting-out rhymes are:

Eeny, meeny, mona, my,
Barcelona, bona, stry,
Kay bell, broken well,
Wee, wo, wack.

Intery, mintery, cutery, corn,
Apple seed, briar thorn,
Wire, briar, limber lock,
Three geese in a flock.
One flew east, one flew west,
One flew over the cuckoo's nest,
O-U-T out!

Monkey, monkey, bottle of beer,
How many monkeys are there here?
One, two, three,
Out goes he (she).

William, William Trembletoe,
He's a good fisherman.
Catches hens, puts them in pens,
Some lay eggs, some lay none.
Wire, Briar, limber lock,
Three geese in a flock,
One flew east, one flew west,
One flew over the goose's nest.
O-U-T spells out and begone,
You old dirty dish rag!

Further Reading

Abrahams, Roger D., and Rankin, Lois, eds. *Counting-Out Rhymes: A Dictionary.* Austin, Tex.: University of Texas Press, 1980.

Bolton, Henry Carrington. *The Counting-Out Rhymes of Children: Their Antiquity, Origin, and Wide Distribution, a Study in Folklore.* 1888. Reprint, Detroit: Singing Tree, 1969.

Goldstein, Kenneth. "Strategy in Counting Out: An Ethnographic Folklore Field Study." In *The Study of Games,* eds. Elliott M. Avedon and Brian Sutton-Smith, pp. 167–178. New York: John Wiley and Sons, 1971.

DICE, KNUCKLEBONES, AND GAMES OF CHANCE

In many cultures, the use of dice in games has been closely related to divination (foretelling the future). The result of throwing dice, which a mathematician would attribute to statistical probability, is interpreted as a message from the gods by gamblers in many cultures. A dice game can consist solely of throwing dice, or the throw of the dice can determine a player's progress in a board game.

Many different objects, both natural and manufactured, have been used as dice. In addition to the familiar six-sided cubes, people have used other geometrical objects with more or fewer sides. The oldest known dice, made over 5,000 years ago, are six four-sided pyramids (three of ivory and three of lapis lazuli) found in the royal tombs of Ur. Seeds, sticks, and seashells that can land on one of two marked sides have also been used. Many Native American games are played with four or more two-sided dice made from peeled and split sticks that are flat on one side and rounded on the other. These dice are used to determine a player's moves in board games, such as the Navajo *Tsidi,* the Chané *Tsúka,* the Paiute *Tatsungin,* the Hopi *Totolospi,* the Yokuts *Tsikehi,* and the Zuni *Sho'liwe.*

In many parts of the world, including Ancient Greece and Rome, the knucklebones of sheep and goats were used in gambling and fortune telling. Children also used them to play games like modern jacks and marbles. A mural at Pompeii shows a girl using knucklebones to play a game of jacks. Among Native American groups in Peru, Bolivia, and Argentina, the knucklebones of cows or llamas have been used in a gambling game called *Taba.*

A knucklebone has six sides, four long rectangles, and two small squares. When it is thrown, it will always land on one of its four long sides and never on one of its two short ends, so there are only four possible results when throwing one knucklebone. Each of the four long sides is slightly different in appearance, and experienced players do not need to mark the sides to tell them apart.

In Ethiopian children's games, the fall of the knucklebone or *tav* is thought to indicate, in a playful way at least, a child's future status in life. There, as in other parts of North Africa and in Armenia, Iran, Greece, and Turkey, the four sides are called king, vizier (advisor to the king), peasant, and slave.

Some of the knucklebone games played by children in Mediterranean countries resemble marble games, but instead of being shot or rolled, knucklebones are spun between the thumb and fingers. These games may be played for keeps, as has been reported for the Moroccan knucklebone game, *Mala.* In other games, such as modern Greek knucklebones, a losing player's knucklebones are returned by the winner with rap on the back of the hand or a similar punishment.

See the following dice, knucklebones, and games of chance in the Games Treasury:

IRAQ: KNUCKLEBONES

UNITED STATES (NATIVE AMERICAN—PIMA): *GINS* (STICKS)

DRAMA AND PANTOMIME GAMES

Until recently, many of the traditional games played by children in Europe and the Americas included miniature dramas, partly ritualized, partly improvised. These games are far less common now than they were 50 years ago. Today, dramatic folk games are more likely to be completely improvised, like charades.

Market Games

In one type of dramatic game that has been widely recorded in Europe and the Americas, two players assume the roles of competing buyers, while a third takes the part of seller or shopkeeper. The remaining players are products for sale, all belonging to a specific category—ribbons, colors, birds, fruits, or vegetables being the most common. In many games, the two buyers are called the angel and the devil, and the drama is followed by a tug-of-war between the forces of good and evil.

See the following market games in the Games Treasury:

COLOMBIA: *LOS LISTONES* (THE RIBBONS)

VENEZUELA: PLANT MARKET

Miming Occupations

Traditional pantomime games played by children include ones in which players imitate workers engaged in various occupations (reported in France, Kenya, and the United States), and players miming musicians playing various instruments (in Morocco, Greece, Germany, and the Netherlands).

See the following miming occupations games in the Games Treasury:

PAKISTAN: *MAZDOORI*

SLOVAK REPUBLIC: TRADES

UNITED STATES: LEMONADE

URUGUAY: *MAN-TAN-TIRU-LIRU-LÁ*

See the following for other drama and pantomime games in the Games Treasury:

RUSSIA: CZAR AND PEASANTS

TANZANIA: GIANT'S HOUSE

FORFEITS

In European and European-American games, there were often penalties, called forfeits, assigned to players who made mistakes. These players had to surrender some item that they were wearing or had with them. At the end of a game, all forfeited items could be gotten back only if the owners performed some difficult or embarassing task. Forfeits have generally fallen out of fashion in children's games today, though children play a game somewhat like forfeits called Truth or Dare. Each player must either answer a question truthfully or be assigned an embarrassing penalty.

In a typical forfeit session from a game played in the United States, one player was appointed judge and blindfolded. Another player held each forfeited item over the judge's head. The player holding the forfeit said, "Here is a forfeit, a very fine forfeit. What shall be done to redeem it?" The judge then asked, "Is it fine or superfine?" (which meant, does it belong to a boy or a girl?). The judge then assigned a forfeit to the owner of the item.

In other versions of forfeits, the entire group decided on the forfeits in the following way: forfeited items were placed underneath a cloth so that only a rough outline of each one could be seen. One player pointed to each forfeit in turn, and the others agreed on the forfeit required to redeem it. Players needed to be careful in assigning forfeits, because the item might be their own!

In Ireland, games of forfeit were often played in earnest: if a player could not perform his forfeit or could not get someone to perform it for him, the forfeited item was tossed into the fireplace.

Here are some examples of forfeits from Irish games:

- Eat a raw potato.
- Chew on a bar of soap.
- Walk barefoot around the outside of the house nine times.
- Stand on your head for 10 minutes.

Some forfeits from the United States are:

- Bow to the prettiest person in the room, kneel to the wittiest, and kiss the one you love best.
- Count backwards rapidly from a given number.
- Hop around the room on one foot.
- Pay a compliment to each person in the room.
- Answer "No" to every question asked of you.
- Kiss every girl (boy) in the room.
- Crawl on all fours and bark like a dog.
- Pick up three coins from the floor with your teeth.

See the following games in the Games Treasury that include forfeits:

FRANCE: THE PRINCE OF PARIS

GERMANY: *ALLE VÖGEL VLIEGEN* (ALL BIRDS FLY)

19

ITALY: ANGELS AND DEMONS

JAMAICA: BECAUSE, YES, AND NO

UNITED KINGDOM (SCOTLAND): ALBERT ADAMS ATE AN ALLIGATOR

UNITED STATES: TWELVE DAYS OF CHRISTMAS

GUESSING GAMES

Guessing games are some of the simplest traditional games and the most widespread. Players of these games do not imagine that their guesses are random. Rather, they are considered tests of observation, intuition, or even clairvoyance.

Who Was It?

One player is blindfolded and must guess the identity of another player, who touches him. Or he might be asked to identify another player by the sound of her voice.

In a guessing game from Finland called *Kauransyöttö*, one player hides her face in the lap of another and puts her hands behind her back, palms upturned. Another player hits her on the hands, and she tries to guess who it is. In Ancient Greece, the person hitting also made a buzzing noise.

In a game from Algeria, one player gets on his knees and hides his eyes. Another player rests his hand on the back of the first. The others place their hands on his, forming a pile of hands. The kneeling player must guess whose hand is touching him.

In some of these guessing games, there is a penalty for guessing incorrectly, such as being spanked by the others. In the case of a correct guess, the player who has been identified assumes the It role.

See the following Who Was It? games in the Games Treasury:

HUNGARY: *DOBI-DOBI*

IRAN: WHO WAS IT?

UNITED STATES: PEGGY IN THE RING

How Many Fingers?

Another ancient and widespread game involves guessing how many fingers someone is holding up behind a player's back. Variations have been found in Argentina, Denmark, England, Ireland, Germany, Italy, Japan, the Netherlands, Norway, Portugal, Scotland, Spain, Sweden, Switzerland, Turkey, the United States, and Wales. In fact, folklorist Paul Brewster identified over 80 different versions of this game in his article, "Some Notes on the Guessing Game, How Many Horns Has the Buck?" It was played in Ancient Rome to the chant, *"Bucca, bucca, quot sunt hic?"* (Buck, buck, how many are here?).

Nearly all of these games are accompanied by a short chant, such as the following from the United States:

Hickety-hack on your poor back,
How many fingers do I hold up?

If the guess is wrong, the guesser is pounded on the back.

See the following How Many Fingers? game in the Games Treasury:

UNITED KINGDOM (WALES): HOW MANY FINGERS?

Who Has It?

In another type of guessing game, one player must guess who is holding a certain object or in which hand a player is holding an object.

See the following Who Has It? games in the Games Treasury:

KOREA: *MEK KONK*

MALAWI: *CHUCHU*

MALI: *SEY*

MOZAMBIQUE: *UMAKE* (THE COAST)

ROMANIA: RINGLET TURNS

UNITED STATES: HEAD OF THE CLASS

UNITED STATES (NATIVE AMERICAN—CHIPPEWA): MOCCASIN GAME

Gesture Anticipation

Some guessing games involve anticipating what sort of motion or sign an opposing player will make. A game of this type, such as when players form their hands into scissors, paper, and stone, is played in many countries.

See the following gesture anticipation games in the Games Treasury:

INDONESIA: MAN, ANT, ELEPHANT

ITALY: *MORRA*

JAPAN: *JAN KEN PO*

LIBERIA: JUMPING GAME

New Zealand (Native Maori): *Hipitoi*

Zambia: Hand-Clapping Game

HAND-CLAPPING GAMES

Clapping hands to songs and rhymes—in pairs, fours or circles—is a popular playground game in the United States. Hand-clapping games are expressive and challenging, as players clap their own hands, their partners' hands, hit their shoulders or thighs, cross their arms, snap their fingers, bump hips, and pantomime actions, all to folk rhymes, new and old.

The sequences of movements players use in hand-clapping games are not easy to describe in words, and so only one simple hand-clapping game is included in the Games Treasury. Because they are so widely played today, hand-clapping games are an excellent resource for teachers and others to use in introducing the subject of traditional games to children and as a focus of collecting projects (see Chapter 4: "Collecting and Exploring Traditional Games"). Hand-clapping is also entertaining for an audience to watch, making it an ideal activity for multicultural festivals and other events where traditional games are presented on stage.

See the following hand-clapping game in the Games Treasury:

United States: Miss Mary Mack

HIDE-AND-SEEK

Hide-and-seek games are played in every part of the world. The game was described by the Roman writer Julius Pollux in the second century A.D. Some of the names for the game in other countries are *Taupunipuni* among the Maori of New Zealand, *Kumukumu* in Papua New Guinea, *El Esconder* in Spain, *Taguán* in the Philippines, *Santakukadi* or *Thappo* in India, *Achgabook* in Armenia, and *De-a Vati Ascuns* in Romania. In the Netherlands, over 300 versions of hide-and-seek have been recorded, each with a different name.

In a typical North American game of hide-and-seek, one player is selected to be It, and a place is chosen as home base. It covers her eyes and counts to 50 or 100, then calls out some words, such as "Ready or not, here I come!," to let the players know she is about to begin looking for them. When It sees a player, she calls his name, saying something like "One, two, three on so-and-so," and runs for home. If It reaches home first, that player is out of the game. If the player reaches home first, he is free. A player who can run to home base and touch it, even without being seen by It first, is also free. The first player out becomes It in the next game.

Every neighborhood has its own special rules for hide-and-seek (such as which hiding places are legal and which are illegal) and its own vocabulary words and phrases. In a hide-and-seek game recorded in Nebraska, It gives the hiders three warnings that he is about to start looking for them:

> All not hid holler "I!"
> A bushel of wheat and a barrel of clover,
> All not hid can't hide over!

and finally says,

> All eyes open, here I come!

Some North American variations of hide-and-seek are Sardines, in which It hides and the others, once they find her, crowd into the hiding place, and Kick the Can (or Kick the Stick), in which players who have been tagged out can be rescued and brought back into the game.

See the following hide-and-seek games in the Games Treasury:

INDONESIA: *SOROK-SOROK*

UNITED STATES (NATIVE AMERICAN—PAMUNKEY): HIDE-AND-SWITCH

Hidden Object

Other types of hide-and-seek games involve hiding an object that one or several players must find. In some games, the players who hid the object assist It by saying "hot," "warm," or "cold" to indicate how close the seeker is to the object. Games of this type have been documented in Hungary, Italy, Nigeria, South Africa, Spain, and Latin America. In the Anglo-American I Spy, the French *Cache-cache,* and the Spanish *Veo, Veo,* an object in plain sight is chosen by the players but not hidden. It must identify the object with the aid of cues from the other players, who tell him what letter the object begins with, for example, or what color it is.

See the following hidden object games in the Games Treasury:

MALAYSIA: *MAIN CHINA BUTA*

MYANMAR (BURMA): GUESSING GAME

PARAGUAY: *EL PAN QUEMADO* (BURNED BREAD)

SENEGAL: *LAGAN BURI*

UNITED STATES (NATIVE AMERICAN—JICARILLA APACHE): RAVEN GOES TO HIS CHILD

Passing an Object around the Circle

The players sit in a circle with It at the center and pass an object in a way that will prevent It from seeing who has it, such as behind their backs, under their knees, or in their closed hands. In some versions, players sing a song, and when the song ends, It must guess who has the object. In other versions, It is allowed to guess the location of the object whenever he chooses. The game is made more exciting when, for instance, skilled players pretend to pass the object while one of them is actually holding onto it. When passing a shoe, a cap, or a belt behind their backs or under their knees, players delight in thumping It on the back with the object when he is looking, mistakenly, toward the opposite side of the circle. This type of game has been documented in Belgium, the Central African Republic, Denmark, England, Ethiopia, Finland, Germany, Greece, Hungary, India, Malaysia, the Netherlands, Sweden, Russia, and throughout North and South America.

See the following passing an object games in the Games Treasury:

GUYANA: RING ON A STRING

IRELAND: PASS THE BROGUE

PAPUA NEW GUINEA: *MAILONG SERA*

RUSSIA: ERMINE

HOPSCOTCH

The "scotch" in hopscotch is an old English word meaning "scratch." Before sidewalks, hopscotch diagrams were scratched in dirt or sand or on stone pavements. Other English words for the game are Beds, Hap the Beds, Hopscore, Hop-crease, and Hickety-hackety. In the United States, the game is called Hopscotch, Potsy, and Sky Blue.

There are many ways to draw a hopscotch diagram, and nearly all of them can be found nearly everywhere the game is played. In other words, there is not a typical French hopscotch diagram and a typical American one and a typical Chinese one. Quite the contrary, as many as 20 different diagrams have been found in just one neighborhood in San Francisco. Snail hopscotch (like *El Caracol* from Argentina in this book) is found worldwide, as are airplane-shaped diagrams and large rectangles divided into six, eight, 10, or more squares.

How big should hopscotch squares be? Players seem to know instinctively: not *too* small, so that there is plenty of room to hop in them without hopping on a line, and not *too* big, so that a player can easily hop from one to the next. Sixteen to 18 inches square is about right, though in some games the squares are actually rectangles that are much wider than they are deep.

Most, but not all, hopscotch games are played with markers. These may be pebbles, flat stones, bits of broken pots, or other objects such as shoe polish tins filled with clay or sand. The marker is usually thrown or pushed into the first square before a player begins the first round of hopping, into the second square before the second round, and so on. The player also performs various actions with the marker, such as picking it up and carrying it out, or kicking it ahead through all the squares as she hops.

Hopscotch rules may also require that players hop around the squares once backward or blindfolded or with the marker balanced on one foot. There may be special words a player uses once or twice to allow him to put down his lifted foot or to move closer to a square when tossing his marker.

There are two ways of winning hopscotch games: completing the required number of rounds first, or owning the most squares at the end of the game. Owning squares is usually accomplished by finishing a certain number of rounds and then tossing the marker into a square and writing one's name on it. Owned squares are off limits to anyone other than their owner, and in some games, the owner must always land on both feet in her square. If she hops on one foot by mistake, she loses ownership.

See the following hopscotch games in the Games Treasury:

ARGENTINA: *EL CARACOL*

BOLIVIA: *LA POLLERÍA*

BOSNIA: *SKOLA* (SCHOOL)

GERMANY: *HINKSPIEL* (HOPSCOTCH)

HAITI: *MARELLES* (HOPSCOTCH)

HONDURAS: *LA RAYUELA*

MEXICO (NATIVE TARASCAN): *PELECHE*

THE NETHERLANDS: WATER HOPSCOTCH

PANAMA: *EL PEREGRINO* (THE PILGRIM)

UNITED KINGDOM (ENGLAND): HOPSCOTCH

UNITED STATES: CATEGORIES HOPSCOTCH

UNITED STATES: "MAY I?" HOPSCOTCH

Further Reading

Lankford, Mary D. *Hopscotch around the World.* New York: William Morrow, 1992.

JACKS

The game of jacks was until recently called "jackstones," which comes from the English "chuckstones," meaning stones for tossing ("chucking"). Jackstones were usually pebbles in England and among English ethnic groups in other countries. Serious players kept a personal collection of them and were always on the lookout for promising new ones. The best pebbles for jackstones are small enough so that five or more can easily be held in a players hand, but not so small that they are difficult to pick up. For games that involve tossing the stones in the air and catching them on the back of the hand, flat stones are best. They should not be round, though, because round pebbles may roll too far when they are scattered for pickup games.

Jacks is a popular sidewalk and floor game in the United States, where it is usually played with a small rubber ball and five to 10 six-pointed metal or plastic jacks that are purchased at a store. Using a rubber ball makes jacks easier than the jackstone games played with rocks, pebbles, and seeds, because players usually wait to catch the ball after one bounce. This gives them more time to perform the required moves and pickups.

Games like jacks were played in Ancient Greece and Rome (paintings of players appeared on Greek vases), and jacks games are played today in every part of the world. Pebbles, beans, bones, grains of corn and other seeds, and small fruits and nuts have all been used as jackstones. Tiny beanbags filled with rice, sand, or beans have been used in Japan and China. In Malaysia and Indonesia, flat seashells are sometimes used, and in Scotland, whelk shells. In India, children play *Sagargote* with beans, and *Chapete* with small, wood cubes painted red and green.

See the following jacks games in the Games Treasury:

AUSTRALIA: JACKSTONES

JAPAN: *OTEDAMA*

KENYA: JACKSTONES

LAOS: JACK STICKS

MALAYSIA: *MAIN SEREMBAM*

MEXICO: *LAS CHIVAS* (BEANS)

MOROCCO: *TABUAXRAT*

RWANDA: *MATHA KISANA* (JACKSTONES)

SOUTH AFRICA: *DIKETO*

TRINIDAD AND TOBAGO: *TRIER*

UNITED STATES: JACKS

United States (Native American—Apache): Jackstones

United States (Native Hawaiian): *Kimokimo*

JUMP-ROPE GAMES

People have been making rope for many thousands of years, and they have been jumping over it for just about as long. In some parts of the world, children still use vines as jump ropes. In England, it used to be traditional after the hop harvest for the harvesters to celebrate by turning a hop vine and jumping over it. Rope skippers often recite folk rhymes as they jump, and thousands of these rhymes have been recorded.

It is possible for one person to jump rope alone, but most jump-rope games involve at least three players, two turning the ends of a 15-to-20-foot-long, fairly heavy rope as the third jumps. The turners establish a rhythm, then jumpers can run through one at a time or jump in and skip to a rhyme. Sometimes a jumper performs pantomime actions to accompany the chant, and most chants end in a series of faster jumps that test a player's skill. Jumpers in Japan and Southeast Asia perform fast jumps from a squatting position. These faster jumps are often performed to fortune-telling rhymes. For example, the jumper asks, "What will I be married in?," then jumps to a repetition of "Silk, satin, calico, rags." The word on which one missed signifies the material of the jumper's wedding clothes.

Another rope game is Chinese Jump Rope. In the United States, this game is played with an elastic rope that can be made from rubber bands, chained and braided to form a circle about 15 feet in circumference. Elastic jump ropes can also be purchased. The rope is stretched in a rectangular shape around two player's legs and is moved higher and higher for some jumps. Chinese Jump Rope has been described as "cat's cradle made with the toes," because players not only jump over the rope, they also catch it in various ways with their feet.

Chiwewi, a game from Nigeria, is an example of another way of jumping over a rope: a player holds one end of a rope that is tied to a soft object and spins the rope around while the other players jump over it.

See the following jump-rope games in the Games Treasury:

Nigeria: *Chiwewi*

Peru: *El Reloj* (The Clock)

United States: Jump Rope

Further Reading

Abrahams, Roger D. *Jump-Rope Rhymes: A Dictionary.* Austin, Tex.: University of Texas Press, 1969.

Boardman, Bob. *Red Hot Peppers: The Skookum Book of Jump Rope Games, Rhymes, and Fancy Footwork.* Seattle: Sasquatch, 1993.

Butler, Francelia. *Skipping around the World: The Ritual Nature of Folk Rhymes.* Hamden, Conn.: Library Professional Publications, 1989.

Skolnik, Peter L. *Jump Rope!* New York: Workman, 1974.

LONDON BRIDGE

Games similar to the English London Bridge, in which two players make an arch with their upraised arms and trap other players who pass beneath, have been recorded across Europe and the Americas, and in parts of Africa and Asia. Most European versions of this game involve players choosing sides for a final tug-of-war. A widespread feature of this tug-of-war is that the two arch players have secret identities, one angelic, the other devilish (this is usually not a part of the English London Bridge). When these two players ask the others to choose between them, the choice seems harmless: players are choosing between oranges or lemons, for instance. When all of the players have chosen a side, they are told which choice they have *really* made, and the final tug-of-war has the significance of a battle between good and evil.

In a London Bridge-type of game from Papua New Guinea, two children make an arch, catch the "bats" that fly underneath, and pretend to carve and eat their captives. As in most non-European versions, there is no tug-of-war.

See the following London Bridge games in the Games Treasury:

CHILE: *LA GALLINA QUE SE VA* (THE RUNNING HEN)

CZECH REPUBLIC: GOLDEN GATE

ITALY: ANGELS AND DEMONS

SUDAN: LEOPARD TRAP

ZIMBABWE: *KANZHINGE*

MARBLES

The Roman Emperor Augustus Caesar was said to have spent many hours of his childhood playing *Nuces,* a children's game resembling marbles but played with round nuts. Nuts are traditionally used in marble games played by Jewish children at Passover. Over the centuries, small, hard balls for game play have been made from marble, glass, limestone, agate, alabaster, the tips of buffalo horns, clay, porcelain, steel, and plastic.

28

Marbles are most often used in simple target games, in which they are shot or rolled into a series of holes dug in the ground. In other games, players put a certain number of marbles within a circle or square and try to knock the other players' marbles out of the circle. In both types of games, play is sometimes for keeps, meaning that players keep the marbles that they capture. It was once common knowledge that an American child's skill at marbles could be judged by the heft of his marble bag.

Marbles was an extremely popular folk game in the United States until about the 1950s or 1960s. The game may have lost popularity because of the disappearance of the ideal playing space: a flat expanse of packed dirt where the marbles rolled well, but not too well. In most American marbles games, players kept shooting from the spot where their marble stopped rolling, as in golf or croquet. On a paved street sidewalk, a marble may roll much *too* far before it stops.

When dirt lots were no longer available, new ways of playing marbles had to be invented. Sidewalk marble games became one-shot target games, in which marbles were lined up against the side of a building and shot at, or marbles were shot at holes cut in the side of a shoebox.

Depending upon the game, marbles may be rolled, tossed, or dropped, but most often they are shot. To shoot a marble, a player must "knuckle down"—place the knuckles of the shooting hand on the ground, grip the marble in the curled forefinger and flick it forward with a quick movement of the thumb.

See the following marbles games in the Games Treasury:

BOLIVIA: *LAS CANICAS* (MARBLES)

CANADA (NATIVE AMERICAN—CREE): *TCOSKUMINA-A* (SLIDING GAME)

IRAQ: KNUCKLEBONES

KOREA: MARBLES

SAUDI ARABIA: MARBLES

UNITED STATES: MARBLES

UNITED STATES (NATIVE AMERICAN—APACHE): MARBLES

UNITED STATES (NATIVE AMERICAN—SHAWNEE): *TETEPAULALOWAAWAA (ROLLING GAME)*

UNITED STATES (NATIVE AMERICAN—SIOUX): MARBLES

Further Reading

Ferretti, Fred. *The Great American Marble Book.* New York: Workman, 1973.

Page, Linda Garland, and Smith, Hilton, eds. *Foxfire Book of Toys and Games.* New York: Dutton, 1985.

This book includes interesting personal accounts of marbles game played in Appalachia in the early part of this century.

Sturmer, Fred, and Seltzer, Adolph. *What Did You Do When You Were a Kid?* New York: St. Martin's, 1973.

The authors describe their own experiences with marbles, both as a game and as a vital part of a child's social life in United States in the 1930s.

MEMORY GAMES

Memory games provide children with an opportunity to develop and display their skill at remembering things they have seen or heard. In an American children's party game, players look at a tray filled with everyday objects. The tray is then covered, and players try to write down the names of all of the objects. In South Africa, children play games in which they look at drawings scratched on the ground or at rows of stones. Then they turn their backs and must be able to answer a series of difficult questions about what they just saw. The South African game *Dithwai* (page 131) is especially interesting because the memory skills used (remembering what stones look like) are directly related to the players' task of herding their families' cattle.

Games that test verbal memory are usually cumulative: players try to repeat, in order, a list of things said by the previous players. Then each one adds something to the list for the next player to remember. An example is the game Grandmother's Attic, played in the United States. Players take turns naming imagined items in granny's attic, each item beginning with a the next letter of the alphabet. Each player must name all the previous items, in order, before adding a new item.

See the following memory games in the Games Treasury:

SOUTH AFRICA: *DITHWAI*

UNITED STATES: TWELVE DAYS OF CHRISTMAS

NUMBER AND COUNTING GAMES

Number and counting games provide training in performing mental calculations quickly and accurately. They are most often played in cultures that have formal education.

See the following number and counting games in the Games Treasury:

ECUADOR: *EL SIETE LOCO* (CRAZY SEVEN)

FRANCE: THE PRINCE OF PARIS

ITALY: *MORRA*

UNITED STATES: FIZZ-BUZZ

Further Reading

Gullen, Doreen F. *Traditional Number Rhymes and Games*. London: University of London Press, 1950.

RACING GAMES

Competitions to see who can go farthest or fastest are at least as old as the Ancient Greek Olympics. In traditional races, runners usually must not only be fast, they must struggle against additional odds. The Native Americans of Central America and the southwestern United States race long distances while kicking a small, hard ball along in front of them. In the United States, children race with both feet inside potato sacks; in Vietnam, children race with their feet inside rice sacks. In Guyana and parts of Brazil, Native Americans hold relay races in which teams carry logs weighing hundreds of pounds.

See the following racing games in the Games Treasury:

BELGIUM: *CHENILLE-ASSIS* (CATERPILLAR SITTING DOWN)

BELGIUM: TUNNEL RACE

ISRAEL: HAT RACE

UNITED STATES (NATIVE AMERICAN—PIMA): *WEE-ICHIDA* (RACING GAME)

UNITED STATES (NATIVE AMERICAN—YUPIK): *UHL-TA* (RING AROUND)

ZIMBABWE: WHISTLING RACE

SHUTTLECOCK

A shuttlecock is a small ball or disc, usually with three or four feathers attached to it in a tuft. The shuttlecock may be batted back and forth between several players or kicked up in the air many times by one person. In some games, the shuttlecock must be kicked with the foot, while in others it is hit with a flat palm or a wooden paddle (called a battledore in English tradition). A modern manufactured game that is played much like the traditional shuttlecock games is Hacky Sack.

Shuttlecock games have been played in Asia for over 2,000 years. Games of this kind are also played by native peoples throughout North and South America. In Japan, hitting a small shuttlecock back and forth with paddles is part of the traditional New Year's celebration. In England, Shrove Tuesday (the day before the beginning of Lent) was once known as Shuttlecock Day in Leicestershire and Yorkshire, and everyone, young and old alike, played with battledores and shuttlecocks. It was said that the number of times a person could hit the shuttlecock without missing predicted how many more years that person would live.

In Tibet, shuttlecocks are made by sticking feathers into a small ball of wool. The native people of South America used a ball made of maize leaves, with or without feathers. Batting a shuttlecock with the palm of the hand was a women's game among the Aztecs.

See the following shuttlecock games in the Games Treasury:

Brazil: *Petéca*

China: Shuttlecock

Thailand: *Takraw*

United States (Native American—Makah): Shuttlecock

SINGING AND CHANTING GAMES

Singing and chanting games, such as the Anglo-American *Here We Go 'Round the Mulberry Bush*, are often short, intricate musical dramas and are difficult to replicate unless one is fortunate enough to find a player who can teach them.

Further Reading

The following are some sources of authentic singing and chanting games that include directions for playing, along with musical notation:

Beckwith, Martha Warren. *Jamaica Folk-Lore.* Memoirs of the American Folklore Society 21 (1928). New York: G.E. Steckert Co.

Gomme, Alice Bertha. *The Traditional Games of England, Scotland, and Ireland; with Tunes, Singing-Rhymes, and Methods of Playing According to Variants Extant and Recorded in Different Parts of the Kingdom.* 2 vols. 1894, 1898. Reprint, New York: Dover, 1964.

Henius, Frank. *Songs and Games of the Americas.* New York: Charles Scribner's Sons, 1943.

Jones, Bessie, and Hawes, Bess Lomax. *Step It Down: Games, Plays, Songs, and Stories from the African American Heritage.* New York: Harper and Row, 1972.

Newell, William Wells. *Games and Songs of American Children.* 2nd ed. 1903. Reprint, New York: Dover, 1963.

Opie, Iona, and Opie, Peter. *The Singing Game.* Oxford: Oxford University Press, 1985.

STORYTELLING AND WORD GAMES

Storytelling, riddling, and word play can be pursued for their own sake, but these activities are also the basis for competitive folk games that test verbal competence and inventiveness.

See the following storytelling and word games in the Games Treasury:

AFGHANISTAN: *MELON*

ANGOLA: RIDDLE CONTEST

JAMAICA: BECAUSE, YES, AND NO

PHILIPPINES: *HEP*

UNITED KINGDOM (SCOTLAND): ALBERT ADAMS ATE AN ALLIGATOR

UNITED STATES: A, MY NAME IS ALICE

URUGUAY: *MAN-TAN-TIRU-LIRU-LÁ*

Further Reading

Lipman, Doug. *Storytelling Games: Creative Activities for Language, Communication, and Composition across the Curriculum.* Phoenix: Oryx Press, 1995.

STRING GAMES

String games have been recorded in nearly every part of the world. Often, the players sing songs as they create the string figures. Among the Inuit of Alaska, a series of string figures that flow one into the next accompanies the telling of a traditional story. Some complicated string figures require the use of hands, feet, and mouth!

In cultures in which string figures are made, children learn to make them by watching and practicing hundreds or thousands of times. Learning to make string figures from a book is a challenge: children can create figures while following the printed instructions, but it takes time and dedication to learn the steps well enough to make the figure from memory.

Further Reading

Gryski, Camilla. *Cat's Cradle, Owl's Eyes: A Book of String Games.* New York: William Morrow Co., 1983.

——. *Many Stars and More String Games.* New York: William Morrow Co., 1985.

——. *Super String Games.* New York: William Morrow Co., 1987.

Jayne, Caroline Furness. *String Figures and How to Make Them: A Study of Cat's Cradle in Many Lands.* 1906. Reprint, New York: Dover, 1962.

TAG AND CHASING GAMES

Running and chasing are activities that come naturally to children. They are an important part of children's play whether or not they are part of a structured game.

Chasing games such as tag channel children's natural inclinations into activities with goals and strategies.

In most of these games, one player is chosen to be the tagger, known as It in English-speaking countries (see Counting Out, page 15). The touch of It has the power to stop, capture, disable, or transfer "It-ness" to a tagged player.

There are many varieties of tag games. Some of the most widely distributed are:

Cat and Mouse

In cat-and-mouse games, one player tries to catch another, and the rest of the players try to prevent the fleeing player from being captured. Usually, the other players form a circle, holding hands. They raise their hands to let the mouse go through and lower them to keep the cat from doing the same. In some games, the cat is required to follow the exact path taken by the mouse. These games are best suited to younger children and are played in China, the Philippines, Russia, most European countries, Canada, the United States, and all of the countries of Latin America.

See the following cat-and-mouse games in the Games Treasury:

COSTA RICA: *EL GATO Y EL RATON* (CAT AND MOUSE)

ITALY: WOLF AND LAMB

Drop the Handkerchief

In games of this type, players sit or stand in a circle, facing inward. The player who is It circles around the outside of the circle, carrying a handkerchief or other small, soft object (usually concealed). It drops the handkerchief behind one of the players and then that player must race It around the outside of the circle. The first player back to the empty space in the circle takes it, and the loser is It for the next game.

See the following Drop the Handkerchief games in the Games Treasury:

CAMBODIA: HANDKERCHIEF GAME

CANADA: DROP THE HANDKERCHIEF

INDIA: *SOTA-PANI*

The two following types of tag are particularly well-suited for play by an older child, who takes the It role, and a group of children who may be too young to play games with complicated rules.

Are You Ready?

One player is chosen to be It. The others ask repeatedly, "What time is it?" or "Are you ready yet?" It improvises answers, such as "Time for me to get out of bed, to brush my teeth, to put on my shirt . . ." and so forth, building suspense, until finally, It shouts "It's DINNER time!" and the chase begins.

See the following Are You Ready? games in the Games Treasury:

PERU: *¿LOBO, YA ESTÁS?* (MR. WOLF, ARE YOU READY?)

UKRAINE: ARE YOU AWAKE, MISTER BEAR?

Line Tag

In this game, the It role usually has the name of a predator animal, and the rest of the players are the prey. One of the prey is a protector, usually the mother or father. The players line up, one behind the other, holding onto the waist, shoulders, or clothing of the player in front. After a short or long discussion, It tries to tag and capture the last player in line, until all have been tagged.

Games like this one are extremely widespread. In Poland, the game is called Gander and Fox; in Russia, Wild Geese; in England, Hen and Chickens or Tom Tiddler's Ground; in the Philippines, Hawk and Chickens; in India, Hawk, Farmer, and Chickens; in Guyana, Hawk and Ducks; in Sudan, Lion and Sheep; in Angola, Leopard and Children; in China, Fox and Geese; and in Zimbabwe, Hen and Wild Cat.

See the following line-tag games in the Games Treasury:

CAMEROON: LEOPARD AND MOTHER HEN

NICARAGUA (NATIVE AMERICAN—MISKITO): JAGUAR GAME

SRI LANKA: CHEETAH AND GOATS

TIBET: WOLF AND SHEEP

TURKEY: FOX AND HEN

UNITED STATES: CHICK-UR-MUR CRAVY CROW

UNITED STATES (NATIVE AMERICAN—COMANCHE): GRIZZLY BEAR

Exchanging Places

In these games, all the players except It have been assigned places. It maneuvers to get two or more players to exchange places, then hurries to get into one of the empty spots.

See the following exchanging places games in the Games Treasury:

AUSTRIA: NUMBERS TAG

CUBA: *EL VENCONMIGO* (COME WITH ME)

DENMARK: THE OCEAN IS STORMY

LEBANON: DO YOU HAVE FIRE?

SWEDEN: NUMBERS TAG

TURKEY: HOW DO YOU LIKE YOUR NEIGHBOR?

UNITED STATES (PUERTO RICO): *POR AQUÍ HAY CANDELA* (HERE IS A LIGHT)

Guarding the Treasure

It attempts to guard an object or objects, while other players attempt to steal them. The player who is It is restricted to a small area and tries to tag the other players.

See the following guarding the treasure games in the Games Treasury:

CAMBODIA: *LEAK PONG KAÈK* (HIDING MOTHER CROW'S EGGS)

IRAN: *BORKUM TOPA* (KICK THE HAT)

JORDAN: TIED-UP MONKEY

UNITED STATES (NATIVE AMERICAN—COMANCHE): GRIZZLY BEAR

Other popular variations of tag include:

Chain Tag: Each tagged player joins hands with It and becomes part of a group It. The two end players can tag others.

Cross Tag: If It is chasing a player, and another player runs between the two of them, It must pursue that player instead. In this way, faster runners can rescue slower ones and make It mad, which is nearly always a goal in It games.

Freeze Tag: Players who have been tagged by It must freeze—stand perfectly still—until freed (tagged) by another player.

Hang Tag: Players cannot be tagged if their feet are off the ground. Traditionally, players of hang tag climbed up into trees. (Parents in India often forbade their children to play this type of tag because of the number of broken bones it caused.) Modern playgrounds offer many safe ways to lift the feet off the ground.

Squat Tag: Players are allowed to squat and thus avoid being tagged. There is a limit to the number of times they can do this, usually three.

Poison Tag: When It tags another player, that player becomes It, and the new It is obliged to hold the spot on her body on which she was tagged as she runs. In this game, It tries to tag others on the foot or another spot that will be difficult to hold while running.

Shadow Tag: In this form of tag, It tries to tag other players' shadows. This game is best played late in the day, of course. Shadow tag also makes a good two-person game: each players tries to tag the other's shadow first.

Touch Wood Tag: Players are safe from being tagged if they touch a certain kind of object or an object made of a certain material, usually wood, iron, or stone, or objects of a particular color.

In addition to the tag games already cited, the following games in the Games Treasury all have tag as a major component:

BANGLADESH: *GUL TARA* (TOSSING TO THE STARS)

GHANA: SNAKE TAG

GREECE: *KUKLA*

INDIA: MAGIC TAG

LIBYA: HOP TAG

PHILIPPINES: *TABIS-TABIS*

SPAIN: MOON AND MORNING STARS

TOGO: *AWAKO* (THE HAWK)

UNITED KINGDOM (ENGLAND): MONDAY, TUESDAY

UNITED STATES: FOX AND GEESE

UNITED STATES (NATIVE AMERICAN—WINNEBAGO): *HAHI'BIDJIKEEUN* (TREE GAME)

VIETNAM: BITING THE CARP'S TAIL

Further Reading

Brewster, Paul G. "Chasing Games." In *American Nonsinging Games*, ed. Paul G. Brewster, 51–77. Norman, Okla.: University of Oklahoma Press, 1953.

TARGET GAMES

Throwing an object at a target is a popular pursuit among people of all ages and all cultures. Games of this type can be easily improvised. Hunting societies have a particular interest in training children to aim accurately. To simulate moving prey, objects such as balls and hoops are rolled along the ground or tossed into the air as children throw spears or shoot arrows at them.

See the following target games in the Games Treasury:

CANADA (NATIVE AMERICAN—CREE): *TIHITPINTOWAN* (ROLLING GAME)

ETHIOPIA: SPEAR THE HOOP

MEXICO: COIN TOSS

NORWAY: THOR'S HAMMER

PORTUGAL: *JOGO DA PEDRA* (STONE GAME)

UGANDA: *INZAMA*

UNITED STATES (NATIVE AMERICAN—KWAKIUTL) *QUAQUATSEWA-IU* (STICK DROP)

UNITED STATES (NATIVE AMERICAN—TETON SIOUX): HOOP AND POLE

UNITED STATES (NATIVE AMERICAN—ZUNI): *TSI-KO-NA* (RING TOSS)

TOPS

Spinning tops have been used as both children's playthings and serious ritual objects in many cultures. In New Guinea, tops have traditionally been used in ceremonies connected with the planting of crops. Adults and children in many parts of the world engage in competitions with fighting tops, trying to hit and damage other players' tops with their own, or trying to knock down objects with tops.

A simple top (often made from a small fruit or nut pierced with a stick) can be made to spin by giving it a twirl between the thumb and fingers. More serious tops are spun by pulling on a cord wound around them. Tops can be kept spinning for a long time by whipping them with a soft leather thong.

Tops races were held in England in the Middle Ages. Each local parish raced its own top down a road on Shrove Tuesday (the day before the beginning of Lent). The tops were kept spinning with whips. After the race, the tops were put away until the following year and said to be sleeping, which is the origin of the phrase, "sleeping like a top."

See the following tops game in the Games Treasury:

PAPUA NEW GUINEA: *TOMONG GILANG BOGL TONDIP* (SINGING TOPS)

TUG-OF-WAR

Games of tug-of-war have been recorded worldwide. Two teams line up on opposite sides of a mark on the ground. The players may all hold onto a long rope, or the head person on each team may each hold onto one of two short sticks tied together with a short piece of rope while the other players hold onto the shoulders or waist of the player in front. Usually, the team that pulls the other team entirely across the mark on the ground is the winner.

Tug-of-war is often played during ceremonial events, where the outcomes are sometimes said to foretell the future. In Korea, the winners of a tug-of-war between neighboring villages could expect to have a good harvest and to be immune to sickness during the following year. In Myanmar (Burma), tug-of-war contests pitted a team representing drought against a team representing rain. Among Native Americans in Alaska, Canada, and the Pacific Northwest, tugs-of-war between people born in summer and people born in winter were thought to predict the severity of the coming winter.

See the following tug-of-war games in the Games Treasury:

CHILE: *LA GALLINA QUE SA VA* (THE RUNNING HEN)

CZECH REPUBLIC: GOLDEN GATE

UNITED STATES (NATIVE AMERICAN—INUIT): DUCKS AND PTARMIGANS

See also London Bridge, page 28.

PART 2
The Games

Chapter 3
Games Treasury

The games in this treasury have been created by generations of children for their own enjoyment. We have tried to select game that are safe and nonviolent when introduced and supervised properly. Some traditional games use natural objects, such as rocks and sticks, that could be dangerous in unskilled hands. Other games have provisions for the winner to thump the loser on the back or rap the loser's knuckles. Adults introducing games should know whether the members of their groups can exercise self-control when given these options. Please preview all games carefully.

We used as many sources as possible, both to verify that a game has been played in a particular country and to give as complete a description of the game as possible. In some cases, we added details from a similar game from a nearby area to make a game's rules complete. Still, users of this book will have to improvise at least some rules. Complete, airtight rules just are not available for most traditional games. This is due in part to the incompleteness of the sources, but also to the very nature of traditional games, whose rules are fluid rather than rigid. We have included suggestions for adapting the rules of some games, based on our experience using these games with children.

Children re-creating these games should be encouraged to work together to explore the possibilities of each game and to add or modify rules in order to make a game work better and to make it more fun.

Game descriptions are written in the present tense; however, many were recorded 50 or more years ago, so the circumstances of play may have changed.

The name of each game is given in the native language when possible, along with an English translation when a reliable one was available. For a great many games, the name has no other meaning in the language. The game given for each country is by no means the "national game." It is simply one of many traditional games that has been played there. We have tried to select games that reflect the area in which they are played—games played with materials unique to the local environment or that include words or phrases in the original language, for example. Finally, we have tried to achieve an overall balance of game types across the collection, so that teachers can locate a variety of games of a specific type (such as tag or hopscotch) for comparative study projects like those in Chapter 4.

For the games in the Games Treasury, we have tried both to describe the traditional playing area and materials and to recommend substitutes as well. For games that require extended playing space, we suggest either a medium-sized playing area, about the size of a classroom, or a large playing area, the size of a school play yard or gymnasium. We have noted with an asterisk (*) games that work best with younger children, ages six through eight. These are games that children nine and older will probably not enjoy. Games that are not specifically recommended for younger children may be beyond their physical or cognitive skills, particularly if you are working with a large group or expecting children to play a new game independently.

Afghanistan
Khana Baudakan

Playing area: A flat, clear space with smooth sand or dirt
Number of players: Two
Materials: Sticks for drawing on the sand or dirt

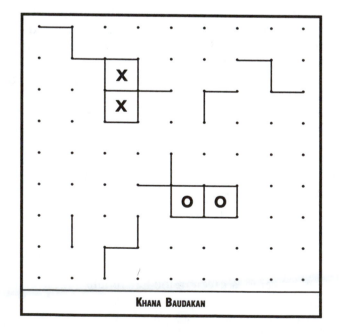

KHANA BAUDAKAN

The players draw a square or rectangular grid of dots on the ground about three inches apart, and they take turns connecting any two dots that are next to each other. Dots may be connected horizontally or vertically, but not diagonally. When one player draws the line that completes a box, she puts an "X" in it and takes another turn. A player will often make many boxes on one turn. The other player will mark his boxes with an "O." Once the entire grid has been turned into boxes and there are no free dots, the player with marks in the most boxes is the winner.

A game very much like this one, Pen the Pig, is played in the United States using pencil and paper. In France, a similar game is called *Pipopipette*. There is no fixed number of dots for the game. A rectangle with 10 to 20 dots on each side is usual. More dots make a game last longer.

Melon

Playing area: A space, indoors or outdoors, where players can sit comfortably

Number of players: Five or more

Materials: None

The players sit in a circle, and one of them begins to tell a story. The story can be either a folktale that everyone knows or a made-up story, but it cannot be a story about something that really happened. When the first storyteller has told a short bit of the tale, he stops suddenly. The next player must continue the story, and so on around the circle. If a player says something that does not make sense, contradicts an earlier part of the story, or cannot think of what to say next, he is out of the game. A player who is out of the game is wrapped in a small carpet, then rolled back and forth several times.

For more information about storytelling and word games and a list of other storytelling and word games in this book, see page 33.

Angola
Riddle Contest

Playing area: In Angola, this game is usually played at night around a fire

Number of players: Two teams of two to four

Materials: Something for marking the score

This game has been played by the Herero people of Angola. Players divide into two teams, and each team chooses a leader. The leaders draw straws to decide who will play first. A player on the first team asks a riddle of the other team. If the other team answers incorrectly, the asking team scores a point. If the other team answers correctly, it becomes that team's turn to ask a riddle, but they do not score a point. Only the asking team can score. The score is kept by marking lines in the dirt. The contest continues until the players begin to fall asleep.

For more information about storytelling and word games and a list of other storytelling and word games in this book, see page 33.

Argentina
El Caracol
(The Snail)

Playing area: Sidewalk, pavement, or hard, flat ground
Number of players: Two or more
Materials: Chalk to mark sidewalk or pavement

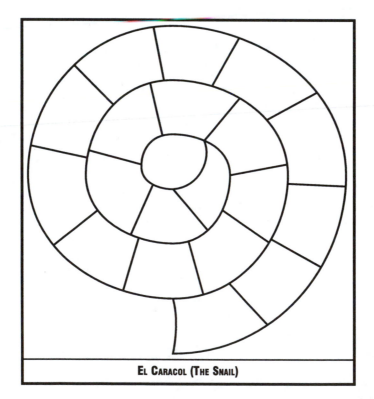

EL CARACOL (THE SNAIL)

In Spanish, *el caracol* means snail or spiral. Spiral hopscotch games like this one are found throughout Europe and the Americas. The players decide how many squares they want in the spiral; a game will last longer if the spiral has more squares. The object of the game is to hop into each square, beginning at the outside, all the way to the center. When a player reaches the center, he turns around, and hops through all the squares in reverse order without ever touching a line. Usually, the rules allow the player to rest on both feet for a while in the center square. A player who completes one round may choose any square and write his name in it. From that time on, only the owner of that square may hop into it, while all other players must hop over it. The owner may also use his square as a resting place. The game ends when so many squares are owned that no one can hop to the center of *el caracol*. The person who owns the most squares wins the game.

For more information about hopscotch and a list of other hopscotch games in this book, see page 25.

Native Araucanian
Pillma

Playing area: A large, clear space, indoors or outdoors
Number of players: Two teams of three to six players each, and two scorekeepers
Materials: Two soft, medium-sized balls or beanbags

All players hold hands and form a circle, then they mark a circle on the ground outside their feet. (In a traditional game, a vine or rope is laid on the ground and used to make the circle.) They mark another line across the circle, dividing it evenly in half. Each team occupies one half of the circle, and each player must stay inside their team's half during play.

The two teams face each other. Using two balls, one player from each team throws one to begin the game. *The ball must always be thrown under one leg.* There are always two balls in play at any time during the game. Players try to hit those on the opposing team with the ball. Players who are targeted try to catch the ball before it touches any part of their body other than their hands. If a player is hit by the ball before she can catch it, a point is scored against her team. A point is also marked against a team if one of its players steps outside the circle, except to retrieve a ball.

One scorekeeper watches each team. The winning team has the lowest score when the game is over. No information is available on how long the game would last. Five or ten minutes is adequate for beginners.

Pillma games have been played by tribes throughout the Pampas and Patagonia regions of South America, where they are traditionally an adult sport as well as a children's game.

For more information about ball games and a list of other ball games in this book, see page 12.

Armenia
Egg Jousting

Playing area: Anywhere

Number of players: Two

Materials: At least one hard-boiled egg for each player

Each player presents an egg to the other, small end up. They then tap the small ends together until one egg cracks. Next they tap the large ends together. The first egg cracked at both ends is surrendered to the opponent.

This game has traditionally been played at Easter in Afghanistan, Armenia, Syria, and Russia, using eggs colored with red dye. Players challenge each other before they begin: "My head can break your head! My heel can break your heel!" (The "head" of the egg is the small end, the "heel" is the larger end.) The challenges continue until the two players are ready to tap their eggs together. Players take this game very seriously, and some misguided youth are reported to have used realistic looking eggs made of china or wood.

The Easter Egg Roll on the White House lawn in Washington, D.C., was originally a competition something like egg jousting. Two children rolled their eggs downhill next to each other, and if one player's egg broke, he gave it to the child whose egg did not break.

Egg Jousting has much in common with Conkers, a game played in the United Kingdom and North America. Players bore a hole through a chestnut, then thread a length of cord, about two feet long, through the hole and tie it. Players twirl the cord and strike their chestnuts together. The player whose chestnuts cracks first is the loser.

See Russia: Egg rolling, for another game that can be played with Easter eggs.

Australia
Jackstones

Playing area: A flat, clear space on floor, dirt, or pavement

Number of players: Two or more

Materials: Five jackstones for each player

The following games are played with five jackstones (pebbles). The one stone that is tossed up into the air is called the "taw," a word that has also been used by jacks players in the United Kingdom, Canada, and the United States. Players take turns trying to complete a game, stopping when they miss. The first player to successfully complete the game without making a mistake is the winner.

Clicks. A player scatters five stones and chooses one as the taw. Next he tosses his taw up in the air, then picks up one stone, clicks it against any other stone and catches the taw—all with the same hand. Now he throws up the two stones he has in his hand, picks up one stone, clicks it against another, then catches two stones he tossed. He has three stones in his hand. He tosses them up, picks up one, clicks it against the last stone, and catches the four. He throws up the four jacks, picks up the last, catches the four, and that's the end.

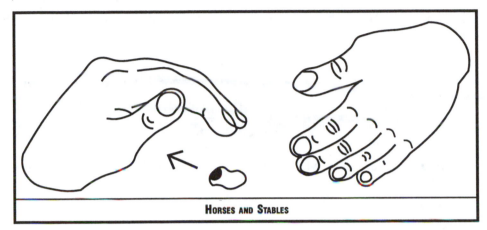

HORSES AND STABLES

Horses and Stables. A player scatters five stones, trying to make them land as close together as possible, then chooses one (usually the farthest one out) as the taw. He cups his left hand (or his right, if he is left-handed) and places it, fingers down, on the ground so that it looks like a little stable with an opening large enough to push a stone inside (the four jackstones are the horses). He tosses the taw straight up into the air, pushes one horse into the stable, then catches the taw before it hits the ground. He does this with the other three horses, as well.

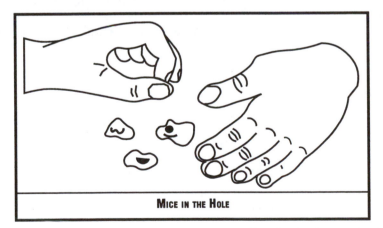

MICE IN THE HOLE

Mice in the Hole. A player tosses five jackstones into the air and tries to catch as many as she can on the back of the same hand. Those that are not caught become the mice for this game. Now, the player chooses a taw from among the stones she caught on her hand. With the other hand, she makes a circle with her thumb and forefinger, with her thumb on the ground (the mouse hole). She tosses the taw, tries to push all the mice into the hole at once, then catches the taw before it hits the ground.

These three games can be played separately or as a series. The first player to successfully complete one game or series of games without making a mistake is declared the winner.

For more information about jacks games and a list of other jacks games in this book, see page 26.

Austria
Numbers Tag

Playing area: A clear space where players can sit in a circle, in chairs or on the ground or floor

Number of players: Fifteen or more

Materials: Blindfold

Players sit in a circle around It, who is blindfolded. Players count off so that each one has a number, which he keeps throughout the game. It calls out two numbers, and the players who have those numbers must run across the inside of the circle and change places. They try not to make any noise, so that It cannot hear them. It tries to tag one of them, and if he does, that player becomes It. When the two players have succeeded in changing places, everyone in the circle claps, which is the signal that It must call out two more numbers.

For more information about tag and chasing games and a list of other exchanging places games in this book, see page 36.

Bangladesh
Gul Tara
(Tossing to the Stars)

Playing area: A clear outdoor space

Number of players: Five or more

Materials: A rubber ball that the players can easily throw straight up and catch. The players throw the ball at each other, so it should be appropriately soft.

One player begins by throwing the ball as high and as straight as possible. The other

50

players try to catch the ball before it touches the ground, and the one who catches it throws it up again. However, if no one catches the ball, the thrower must pick up the ball and then tag another player (by touching or by throwing). The tagged player becomes the new thrower. This game is also popular in India.

For more information about ball games and a list of other ball games in this book, see page 12. For more information about tag and chasing games and a list of other tag and chasing games in this book, see page 37.

Belgium
*Chenille-assis
(Caterpillar Sitting Down)

Playing area: A large indoor or outdoor space (if outdoors, the game should be played on grass)

Number of players: Six or more, in two or more equal teams. A referee or judge may be needed to make sure each team follows the rules.

Materials: None

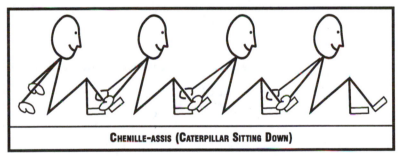

CHENILLE-ASSIS (CATERPILLAR SITTING DOWN)

This is a race between two or more teams, each with an equal number of players, at least three. Players mark a starting line and a finish line, about 20 to 40 feet apart (closer for younger children, further apart for older ones). The members of each team sit on the floor or grass, one behind the other, with knees raised and feet flat on the ground. Each person holds the ankles of the person in back. Teams will need to experiment and decide together how they can move the fastest, and will need some time to practice.

During the race, if any player lets go of an ankle, that team is disqualified. The first caterpillar whose whole team crosses the finish line is the winner.

A similar game is played in Zaire, but it is done for fun, not as a race. Children try to move as fast as they can through tall grass, like a snake.

For more information about racing games and a list of other racing games in this book, see page 31.

*Tunnel Race

Playing area: A medium-sized, clear space, indoors or outdoors
Number of players: Two teams of eight to fifteen players each, and a starter
Materials: A ball, about the size of a soccer ball, for each team

Players divide into two equal teams. The players on each team stand one behind another, legs apart. At a signal, the first player of each team rolls the ball backwards between her legs. The ball should roll all the way to the last player by itself. If the ball rolls out of the tunnel, it must be brought back to the place it rolled out, and that player must push it backward through the tunnel again. The last player catches the ball and runs to the front of the line, then passes the ball backwards between his legs, and so on. The first team to have its first player return to the front of the line is declared the winner.

Two variations of this game are "Kangaroo," in which the player at the back of the line holds the ball between her knees and hops to the front of the line, and "Goat," in which the last player gets on his hands and knees and butts the ball with his head as he crawls to the front of the line. Players could easily invent other ways of moving to the front of the line.

For more information about racing games and a list of other racing games in this book, see page 31.

Bolivia

Las Canicas
(Marbles)

Playing area: A small, clear dirt area
Number of players: Two
Materials: Several marbles for each player

LAS CANICAS (MARBLES)

Players draw a circle, about six inches in diameter, on the ground. One player places a marble in the center of the circle, and the other tries to shoot it out. He stands about three feet away from the circle, lifts up one knee, and places his hand and his marble on it. From his knee, he shoots his marble at his opponent's marble in the circle. If he knocks it out of the circle, he keeps the marble. If he does not, the other player has a turn to shoot, and a chance to win her opponent's marble. When one player knocks a marble out of the ring, the other player must put another in its place, and whenever a player misses, the other takes a turn.

For more information about marbles and a list of other marbles games in this book, see page 29.

La Pollería

Playing area: Sidewalk, pavement, or hard, flat ground
Number of players: Two or more
Materials: Chalk to mark sidewalk or pavement; a flat marker for each player

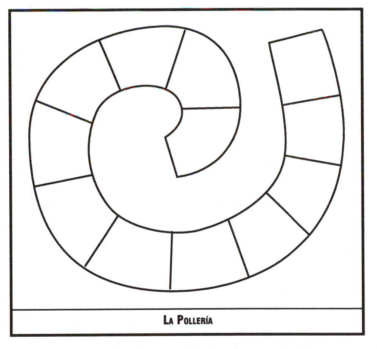

LA POLLERÍA

The first player places her marker just outside the hopscotch diagram (see illustration), kicks it into the first square, and hops on one foot into the first square. She then kicks the marker into the second square, hops into the second square, and so on. She kicks the marker all the way to the center square and back out again. A player loses her turn if she steps on a line, puts two feet down, or fails to kick the marker into the next square. The marker may not land on a line, either. The first player to successfuly hop to the center and back is the winner.

For more information about hopscotch and a list of other hopscotch games in this book, see page 25.

Bosnia

Skola

(School)

Playing area: Sidewalk, pavement, or hard, flat ground

Number of players: Two or more

Materials: Chalk to mark sidewalk or pavement; a flat marker for each player

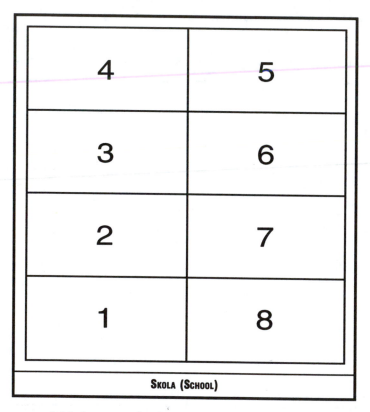

SKOLA (SCHOOL)

The eight squares of this hopscotch represent eight classrooms or grades in a school. Each player uses a flat piece of stone or tile, called a *plova,* as a marker. A complete game consists of eight rounds. In round one, a player tosses her *plova* into square one (first grade), hops into square one, picks up the *plova,* and hops through the rest of the squares in order, finishing at eight and hopping out. In the next round, the player tosses her marker into second grade, then hops through each square as in round one, stopping enroute to pick up her *plova*, and so on. Each player continues playing until she misses the correct square when tossing the *plova,* hops on a line, or puts both feet down. When she makes a mistake, she loses her turn, but may begin her next turn at the same grade level where she made her mistake.

In some versions of the game, the players continue to play for three more rounds after the initial eight. In the first, they hop through all eight squares carrying the *plova* on a raised foot. In the next round, they balance it on top of their heads, and finally they hop one round blindfolded.

For more information about hopscotch and a list of other hopscotch games in this book, see page 25.

Brazil
Luta de Galho
(Cockfight)

Playing area: A medium-sized, clear space, indoors or outdoors
Number of players: Two
Materials: Two scarves or similar squares of fabric

LUTA DE GALHO (COCKFIGHT)

Players mark a circle, about eight or nine feet in diameter, on the ground. Each player puts a scarf in his belt at his right side, so that most of it hangs free. Players balance on one foot and grab the other foot with the opposite hand behind their backs.

The object of the game is for one player to steal the other's handkerchief. A player who hops outside the circle or lets go of his foot or falls is disqualified. The game is usually played in elimination rounds, with winners playing each other until one is proclaimed the champion.

Fighting between two roosters is a favorite adult gambling game in countries around the world. In many of these countries, such as the Philippines, Peru, and the islands of the Caribbean, children play games in which they pretend to be fighting roosters. In some of these games, players squat down and clasp their hands under their knees and try to push one another out of the circle.

Petéca

Playing area: A medium-sized, clear outdoor space

Number of players: Two to ten

Materials: A *petéca,* a small cloth or leather bag filled with sand or grain; three or four six- to eight-inch-long feathers, which are stuck into the top of the bag

A fast way to make a *petéca* is to cut a four-inch circle of lightweight cloth and place a walnut-sized piece of non-hardening clay in the center. Push the quills of several feathers into the clay, then gather the cloth up around the quills and wrap tightly with cord. Another way to make a *petéca* is to stuff a small bag with sand or grain. Coat the quills of the feathers with white glue and push them into the seam of the bag.

A group of children play this game in a circle. One of them tosses the *petéca* into the air, and the players take turns hitting it upwards with the palm of one hand. They may not catch the *petéca,* but must keep their hands open and flat. A player may not hit the *petéca* twice in a row. Sometimes players recite the alphabet as they play, one letter for each hit of the *petéca.*

For more information about shuttlecock games and a list of other shuttlecock games in this book, see page 32.

Bulgaria
Gaping

Playing area: A space, indoors or outdoors, where all players can sit on the ground or floor

Number of players: Six or more

Materials: A stick, about three feet long; a string, also about three feet long, tied to one end of the stick; a piece of candy tied to the end of the string (hard candy in a wrapper works best)

All the players sit in a circle with their hands behind their backs, while one person stands at the center. The person in the center holds the stick and turns around, dangling the candy above the players, who try to catch it in their mouths without using their hands and without standing up. Those who have watched this game report that everyone looks very funny!

This game is played on the night before the beginning of Lent, the period of fasting before Easter. During Lent, many Christians have traditionally given up eating rich foods or sweets, so this game is appropriately symbolic of children's feelings at this time.

Cambodia
Handkerchief Game

Playing area: A clear space, indoors or outdoors
Number of players: Ten or more
Materials: A handkerchief or scarf, knotted at one corner

One player is chosen to be It. The other players sit in a circle, facing the center. (In southeast Asia, children will usually squat rather than sit, which makes it easier for them to rise quickly.) It walks around the outside of the circle carrying a handkerchief, and when he thinks that a particular player is not paying attention, he stealthily drops the handkerchief behind that player, who must pick up the handkerchief and race It around the circle. Both players try to claim the empty place in the circle where the player was sitting. The player who is left out of the circle at the end of the race becomes It for the next round. If It drops the handkerchief behind one of the players and is able to run a complete circle without that player noticing that the handkerchief is behind her, It is allowed to pick up the handkerchief and hit that player on the back with it several times. Everyone laughs at the player who was so incredibly inattentive. Then that player becomes It.

For more information about tag and chasing games and a list of other drop the handkerchief games in this book, see page 34.

Leak Pong Kaèk
(Hiding Mother Crow's Eggs)

Playing area: See game directions below
Number of players: Four or more

Materials: Three or four egg-sized stones are traditionally used; sneakers are both safer and easier for mother crow to find

Players mark off a circle about five feet across as the mother crow's nest. They also mark the boundaries of a larger playing space for the hide-and-seek part of the game.

Players draw straws to determine who is the mother crow. The mother crow gets onto her hands and knees in the center of the circle, placing the stones beneath her, as her eggs. The other players try to get the eggs away without the mother crow tagging them. The mother crow can tag any part of a player's body that is inside the circle, and if she does so, that player must take her place.

If the other players succeed in stealing all of her eggs without being tagged, the mother crow is blindfolded, and the eggs are hidden within the boundaries of the playing space. The mother crow is allowed a certain amount of time to find them. If she does not find them all, the other players grab her by the ears and lead her to the remaining hiding places. Then she must be the mother crow in the next game as well. However, if she does find all the eggs within the time allowed, a new mother crow is chosen by drawing straws.

It is only possible for the players to steal the eggs if they cooperate to distract the mother crow. Older children are better at devising ways to do this—strategies often dictated by the mother crow's unique personality—than younger children.

For more information about tag and chasing games and a list of other guarding the treasure games in this book, see page 36.

Cameroon
Leopard and Mother Hen

Playing area: A large space, indoors or outdoors

Number of players: Six or more

Materials: None

Two players are chosen to be the leopard and the mother hen (usually the oldest and most skillful players). The other players, the chickens, line up behind the mother hen, each one holding the waist or shoulders of the one in front. The leopard stands in front of the mother hen, growling and making catlike motions. The mother hen says, "The leopard is coming to get you!" and the chickens reply, "Poor little chicks, poor little chicks!" Then the leopard roars and runs and tries to tag the last chick in line. Tagged chicks are out of the game, and the leopard tries to catch them all.

This game works best with a mixed-age group.

For more information about tag and chasing games, and a list of other line tag games in this book, see page 35.

Canada
Drop the Handkerchief

Playing area: A clear space, indoors or outdoors, where children can stand in a circle about two feet apart from each other

Number of players: Ten or more

Materials: A handkerchief or scarf

Players stand in a circle, facing inwards. One player is chosen to be It, and he takes the handkerchief in his hand and runs around the outside of the circle. The players in the circle sing,

> I wrote a letter to my love,
> And on the way I dropped it.
> A little puppy picked it up,
> And put it in his pocket.

As he runs behind each player, It says, "I won't bite you, I won't bite you, I won't bite you. . . ." When he decides it is time to drop the handkerchief (usually when he sees a player who is not paying attention), he says, "But I *will* bite you!" Then he drops the handkerchief and runs. That player must stoop down, pick up the handkerchief, and race around the circle in the same direction It is running. Both try to claim that player's empty spot in the circle. If It beats the player, that player becomes It. If not, It must try again.

For more information about tag and chasing games and a list of other drop the handkerchief games in this book, see page 34.

Native American—Cree
Tcoskumina-a
(Sliding Game)

Playing area: A slight downhill slope on snowy ground

Number of players: Two or more

Materials: Marbles or similar round objects

Players prepare a gently sloping track, about five feet long and two feet wide, in the snow. Then they ice the track by spraying it or mopping water over it and allowing the water to freeze. Next they make 12-inch-deep holes, each about three times as wide as a marble, across the bottom end of the course. Players decide whether the holes will have the same point value or different point values. Players roll their marbles down the track and score points depending on which hole marbles lands in. The most valuable Cree marbles were traditionally made by cutting off and rounding the tips of buffalo horns.

For more information about marbles and a list of other marbles games in this book, see page 29.

Tihitpintowan
(Rolling Game)

Playing area: A large, flat, open space

Number of players: Two equal teams of three or more

Materials: A hoop, about a foot in diameter (rattan hoops are available in crafts stores); a spear (such as a three-foot-long hardwood dowel) for each player

TIHITPINTOWAN (ROLLING GAME)

This game was best played in the spring after the snow has melted but while the ground is still hard. The hoop is made from willow twigs with a netting of leather thongs or fiber cords covering the inside. Each player has a short spear. A member of one team rolls the hoop along the ground parallel to a line of throwers from the other team. The distance between the throwers and the hoop should vary according to players' abilities. When a player's spear pierces the netting in the hoop, he picks up the hoop and runs after his opponents, trying to tag one of them with it. A player who is tagged with the hoop must leave the game. After one player is tagged, the teams change places. The last player on a team to be tagged by the hoop loses the game for his team.

For more information about target games and a list of other target games in this book, see page 38.

Chile
*Cielo, Luna, Mar
(Sky, Moon, Ocean)

Playing area: Any stairway with at least three steps and wide enough for all the players to stand side by side

Number of players: Three or more
Materials: None

The bottom step is the ocean, the second step is the moon, and the third step is the sky. One person is chosen as the caller, and the other players line up on the third step. The caller says "sky," "moon," or "stars," in any order he wishes, and the other players must jump to the correct step immediately. Any player who jumps to the wrong step is out of the game. The game ends when only one player is left, and that player becomes the new caller.

La Gallina Que Se Va
(The Running Hen)

Playing area: A medium-sized space, indoors or outdoors
Number of players: Ten or more
Materials: None

Two players are selected to form an arch with their arms, as in London Bridge. The two of them decide on a category, such as flowers, colors, or fruits; each of the two chooses a name from that category, but they do not disclose them to the other players. The remaining players line up one behind the other, placing their hands on the shoulders or waist of the one in front. They run around the playing area chanting,

> *Pa! Pa! Pa!*
> *La gallina que se va!*

Then they run through the arch, and the two players bring down their arms and try to catch the last runner in line. When they do, they ask her to choose between their two names. She whispers her choice to them, and they tell her to line up behind whichever one of them she has chosen. This continues until all the players have been trapped and chosen sides. The game ends in a tug-of-war.

For more information about London Bridge and a list of other London Bridge games in this book, see page 28. For more information about tug-of-war and a list of other tug-of-war games in this book, see page 39.

China
*Calling the Chickens

Playing area: A medium-sized, clear space, indoors or outdoors
Number of players: Five or more
Materials: A blindfold

One player is blindfolded and plays the part of the owner of a flock of chickens. The blindfolded player calls to the others, "Come home, my little chickens, come home."

Then all the other players must run forward, and each one must touch the blindfolded player without being tagged. The first chicken to be tagged becomes the next owner.

For more information about blindfold games and a list of other blindfold games in this book, see page 13.

Shuttlecock

Playing area: A clear space, indoors or outdoors
Number of players: One or more
Materials: A shuttlecock (see instructions below)

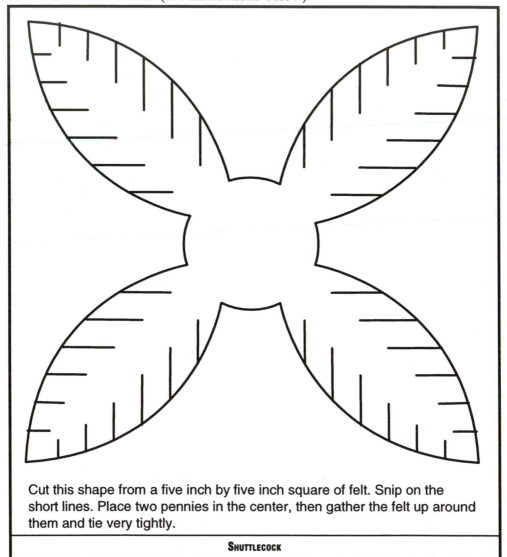

Cut this shape from a five inch by five inch square of felt. Snip on the short lines. Place two pennies in the center, then gather the felt up around them and tie very tightly.

SHUTTLECOCK

Foot juggling with a shuttlecock has been a popular game in China for over 2,000 years. There are two ways to play: several people can stand in a circle and kick the shuttlecock to one another, or one person can juggle it alone. The goal in either form is to keep the shuttlecock from touching the ground for as long as possible. Playing with a number of people in a circle makes it a cooperative game, with all players working to keep the shuttlecock in the air.

A good player can keep the shuttlecock in the air for 200 kicks or more when playing alone. Beginners should try to hit the shuttlecock with the inside (instep) of the foot, aiming it straight up. Advanced players learn to kick the shuttlecock straight up with any part of either foot, and onlookers may call the part of the foot with which the player should kick the shuttlecock, such as "with the toes," or "with the outside of the foot."

Traditional Chinese shuttlecocks are small cloth or leather sacks filled with clay or sawdust and topped with several pheasant feathers. Sometimes shuttlecocks were made by attaching the feathers to the hole in an old Chinese coin.

You can make your own shuttlecock with two pennies, a five-inch square of felt, and a piece of thin ribbon or string. Cut the felt as shown in the illustration. Tape the pennies together and place them in the center of the felt, then tie tightly just above the pennies. Your shuttlecock should always land on its bottom, with the feathery parts sticking up.

For more information about shuttlecock games and a list of other shuttlecock games in this book, see page 32.

Sz'kwa

Playing area: Anywhere

Number of players: Two

Materials: A piece of paper or other flat surface on which to draw the diagram (in China, children often draw it in on the ground); an equal number of markers,

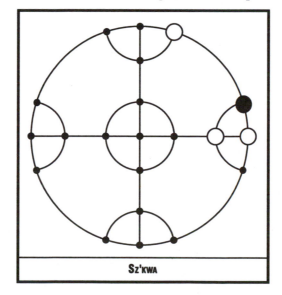

SZ'KWA

but at least twenty, for each player (pebbles, beans, or other small objects may be used, as long as each player uses a different color)

Players take turns placing one marker at a time on any of the points where lines and circles intersect. If the first player's move traps one of the second player's markers—if each one of the points adjacent to the second player's marker is occupied by one of the first player's markers—the first player removes the second player's marker from the board. In the illustration, the black marker is trapped. The game ends when one player has no more markers, or when a player cannot put a marker on the board without being immediately trapped. The winner is the player who has captured the most markers at the end of the game.

For more information about board games and a list of other board games in this book, see page 14.

Colombia
*Los Listones
(The Ribbons)

Playing area: A medium-sized, open space, indoors or outdoors
Number of players: Ten to twenty
Materials: None

Three players are chosen to play the roles of shopkeeper, angel, and devil. Each of the remaining players secretly chooses a color. Or someone whispers the name of a color to each player; this can make the game last longer because it assures that there will be many different colors chosen.

The game begins with the following ritual exchange between the angel and the shopkeeper:

> Angel (pretending to knock on the shop door): Hello.
> Shopkeeper: Who is there?
> Angel: The angel.
> Shopkeeper: What can I do for you?
> Angel: I want ribbons.
> Shopkeeper: What color do you want?

The angel names a color, and the player or players who have chosen that color join him. Then the angel chooses another color. If the angel names a color and no child comes forward, it is the devil's turn, and so on, until all the players are on one side or another. The winning side (good or evil) can be decided by counting who has the most "ribbons" or by a tug-of-war between the two sides.

For a similar game, see Venezuela: Vegetable Market. For other games that include a tug-of-war between good and evil, see London Bridge, page 28. For more information about drama and pantomime games and a list of other market games in this book, see page 18.

Costa Rica
*El Gato y el Raton
(Cat and Mouse)

Playing area: A large, clear space, indoors or outdoors
Number of players: Seven or more
Materials: None

Two players are chosen to be the cat and the mouse. The other players form a circle and hold hands. The mouse stands inside the circle, and the cat stands outside, and everyone sings,

> *Allá viene el gato y el ratón*
> *A darle combate al tiburón.*

(This means "the cat and rat are coming to fight the shark," which, like many folk game chants, does not make much sense but does rhyme.)

The cat tries to catch the mouse while the children in the circle do all they can to keep this from happening. For example, they move close together so the cat cannot get through, or they lower their hands to form a barrier. If the cat gets into the circle, the children lift their arms to help the mouse get out. When the cat has caught the mouse, two new players take their places.

For more information on tag and chasing games and a list of other cat-and-mouse games in this book, see page 34.

Croatia
Jack, Where Are You?

Playing area: A clear space around a post or tree
Number of players: Two, and an audience of potential players
Materials: A rope, about fifteen feet long; a small towel, such as a dish towel; a blindfold

Two players are chosen to be the master and his servant, Jack. The center of the rope is tied to the post at waist height. The master and Jack each hold onto an end of the rope and must not let go during the game. The master is blindfolded and holds a towel in his free hand. When the master says, "Jack, where are you?" Jack must always answer, "Here I am." The game continues until the master succeeds in hitting Jack with the towel, then their roles are reversed. After that, other children take turns playing the roles of the master and Jack.

For more information about blindfold games and a list of other two-person blindfold games in this book, see page 13.

Cuba
*El Venconmigo
(Come with Me)

Playing area: A large, flat space, indoors or outdoors, where players can sit comfortably on the floor or ground

Number of players: Twenty or more

Materials: None

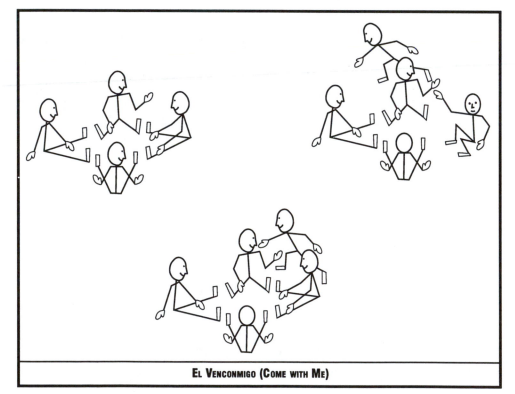

EL VENCONMIGO (COME WITH ME)

Players get into groups of four, and two to five extra players are rovers. Each group of four sits in a circle on the floor or ground, with their legs stretched out straight in front of them and their feet nearly touching, like the spokes of a wheel. The rovers walk or skip around the groups. A rover tries to get into a group by tapping a seated player on the shoulder. Both must then run clockwise around that group of four, and the first one back at the empty place joins that group. The one left out becomes a rover.

For more information about tag and chasing games and a list of other exchanging places games in this book, see page 36.

Czech Republic
*Golden Gate

Playing area: A medium-sized, open space, indoors or outdoors

Number of players: Ten to twenty

Materials: None

Two players are chosen to form an arch with their joined hands, as in London Bridge. Before the game begins, these two decide secretly which one will be the angel and which one will be the devil. The remaining players line up and pass under the bridge as they chant the following:

> Players: Please let us through the Golden Gate.
> Gate: What will you give us?
> Players: Bread and butter, and keep the next one through.

The next player is trapped as the gate is lowered. She is asked to choose whose side she wants to be on, and names one of the two players forming the arch. Then she goes and stands behind that person. The game continues until every player has been captured and has chosen a side. The angel and devil then reveal their identities, and a tug-of-war follows between good and evil.

For more information about London Bridge games and a list of other London Bridge games in this book, see page 28. For more information on tug-of-war and a list of other tug-of-war games in this book, see page 39.

Dahomey
*Godo

Playing area: A sandy area

Number of players: Two or more

Materials: A thin stick, about fourteen to sixteen inches long, for each player; a piece of thin, stiff rope about eight inches long, tied to form a circle

Someone who will not be playing the game hides the circle of rope in the pile of sand. The players push their sticks slowly and carefully down into the sand and try to lift out the concealed rope.

In a similar game from Korea, a finger ring is hidden in a pile of sand, and players dig for it with long, thin sticks.

Denmark
The Ocean Is Stormy

Playing area: A medium-sized space, indoors or outdoors

Number of players: Twelve or more

Materials: A place for each player but one (if there is an odd number of players) or two (if there is an even number), as in a game of musical chairs (make a circle of chairs, or draw a circle for each player but one to stand in)

One or two children are chosen to be It (depending on whether there is an odd or even number of players). They are called the whale or whales. The other children pair off, and each pair decides secretly on the name of a fish. Then the players take chairs or places in the circle. The whale begins to "swim" around the circle, calling out the names of different kinds of fish. As each pair's name is guessed, they get up and follow behind the whale. After all the fish have been guessed (or when the whale cannot think of any new fish names), the whale calls out, "The ocean is stormy!" Everyone rushes quickly to grab a seat, and the player or players who fail to find a place become the whales for the next game.

For more information about tag and chasing games and a list of other exchanging places games in this book, see page 36.

Ecuador
El Siete Loco
(Crazy Seven)

Playing area: A clear space where players can sit in a circle in either chairs or on the floor or ground

Number of players: Five or more

Materials: None

One player begins counting, *uno,* and the player to his left continues, *dos.* When *siete,* or any multiple of seven is reached, all players must clap their hands, and the direction of counting is reversed. Players who fail to clap on a multiple of seven, or who clap on the wrong number, are out of the game. The game may be made more difficult if the players count faster.

For more information about memory games and a list of other number and counting games in this book, see page 30.

Seega

Playing area: Anywhere

Number of players: Two

Materials: Any flat surface on which to draw the game board; three markers for each player

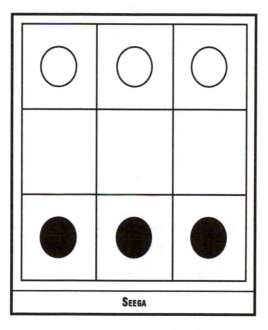

SEEGA

This is a traditional but simplified version of *Seega*. The adult version is played on a board of 25, 49, or 81 squares with markers that total one less than the number of squares. Beans or small stones are traditionally used as game markers and are called *kelbs* (dogs). *Seega* is related to the ancient Egyptian game of *Senet*. The precise rules for *Senet* have been lost, but it is known to have been played in Egypt 5,000 years ago. *Senet* boards were found in the tomb of Pharoah Tutankhamon.

To play children's *Seega,* players set their pieces on the board as pictured in the diagram. They take turns moving one of their markers either one or two squares in any direction. A marker may not pass over another. The winner is the first player to get three markers in a straight line across, down, or diagonally, so long as it is not in the player's original line.

For more information about board games and a list of other board games in this book, see page 14.

El Salvador
La Gallina Ciega
(The Blind Hen)

Playing area: A medium-sized, clear space, outdoors or indoors

Number of players: Five or more

Materials: A blindfold

Players set boundaries for the playing area. One player is chosen to be It and is blindfolded and spun around three times. As the game begins, the other players join hands and circle around the hen, reciting the following:

> Players: Little hen, what are you looking for?
>
> Hen: A thimble and a needle.
>
> Players: We have it, but we won't give it to you.

The hen must then try to tag another player, who will take her place as the blind hen. The other players do not just hide from the blind hen. Much of their enjoyment comes from letting the hen know with their voices that they are close by.

This game, with the same name, is found in Spain and throughout Latin America.

For more information about blindfold games and a list of other blindfold games in this book, see page 13.

Ethiopia
Spear the Hoop

Playing area: A large, clear outdoor space

Number of players: Three or more

Materials: A hoop about twelve to eighteen inches in diameter (rattan hoops may be purchased at crafts stores); a fairly harmless straight stick for each thrower to use as a spear. (A three-foot hardwood dowel works well. Paint or mark the spears with different colors so that players will know which spear hit the hoop.)

Players create a 30- to 40-foot-long pathway down which the hoop will roll smoothly. A player stands at each end of the path while all the others line up, side by side, 10 to 15 feet back from the hoop's path. As the hoop rolls past, they try to throw their spears in a way that will stop the hoop.

For more information about target games and a list of other target games in this book, see page 38.

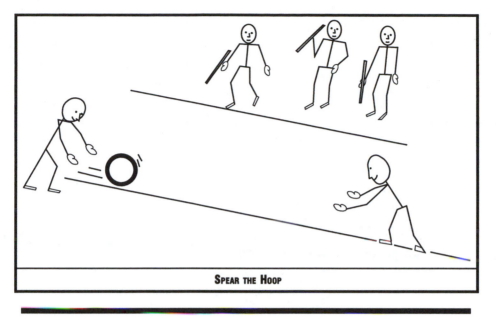

SPEAR THE HOOP

Finland
Steak

Playing area: A small space, indoors or outdoors

Number of players: Four to ten

Materials: Ten to twenty broom straws or drinking straws; a piece, about two feet long, of light rope (or substitute heavy yarn for safety)

This game was traditionally played at Christmas time in Finland. One player is chosen to be It and sits blindfolded, holding the rope in one hand and grasping the straws firmly but lightly in the other hand. The other players try to take the straws, one by one, without It hitting them with the rope, called the *"steak."* Any player hit by the *steak* becomes It. In Sweden, a similar game is called *Nappa Stek,* or "pinch the *steak*." Players try to pinch It, who must then guess who pinched him.

For more information about blindfold games and a list of other blindfold games in this book, see page 13.

France
Les Grelots
(Bell Tag)

Playing area: A medium-sized, clear area, indoors or outdoors, about the size of a classroom, with no dangerous obstacles

Number of players: Five to fifteen

Materials: Bells sewn to one or two Velcro or elastic bands (or use the musical bells that come with rhythm band sets); blindfolds for all players but one

One player is selected to be It. He wears the bells on one or both ankles, or holds the bells in his hands. All the other players are blindfolded. At a signal, the blindfolded players try to catch It, who must keep the bells ringing continually. No running is allowed. When a player catches It, the two change places.

This was once a very popular game in England and was often played at medieval country fairs. The "jingler" would win a prize if he could evade the other players for a certain amount of time.

For more information about blindfold games and a list of other blindfold games in this book, see page 13.

The Prince of Paris

Playing area: Any space where players can sit in a circle

Number of players: Ten to fifteen

Materials: None

Players sit in a circle, and one of them begins by saying, "The Prince of Paris has lost his hat. Did you find it, number three, sir?" The third person clockwise from the first answers immediately:

> Third: What, sir, I, sir?
> First: Yes, sir, you, sir.
> Third: Not I, sir.
> First: Who then, sir?
> Third: Five, sir. (The player can choose any number between one and 15.)

The person who is five places clockwise must then answer, "What, sir, I, sir?" and so on.

Each player's number, relative to the speaker, is always changing, so this is a challenging game even for older children. Any player who does not respond right away, or who answers to the wrong number, must leave the circle or pay a forfeit (see Forfeits, page 18).

In a simpler version of this game from the United States, the players are each given the name of a color when the game begins, and they use these colors throughout the game, for example:

> First speaker: The Prince of Paris has lost his cap. Did you find it, yellow cap, sir?
> Yellow: What, sir, I, sir?
> First: Yes, sir, you, sir.
> Yellow: Not I, sir.

First: Who then, sir?
Yellow: Red cap, sir.

. . . and so on.

Versions of this game are played in England, Germany, Jamaica, the Philippines, and Scotland.

For for more information about memory games and a list of other number and counting games in this book, see page 30.

Germany
Alle Vögel Vliegen
(All Birds Fly)

Playing area: A space, indoors or outdoors, where players can sit in a circle
Number of players: Six or more
Materials: None

One player is chosen to lead the game. The other players sit or stand, ready to flap their arms twice after the leader names an animal, an imaginary being, or anything else that flies. The leader speaks quickly and flaps after everything he names, saying, for example, "All birds fly (flap, flap), all mosquitos fly (flap, flap), all airplanes fly (flap, flap), all porcupines fly (flap, flap)." Any player who flaps his arms at the wrong time, or who fails to flap his arms when he should, must place something small he is wearing or carrying on the floor or table. Once the pile contains many items, it is covered with a cloth and a forfeit game begins. (See Forfeits, page 18.)

Games like this one are played in Chile, Estonia, Finland, Ireland, Jamaica, the Netherlands, Norway, and the United States.

For more information on category games and a list of other category games in this book, see page 15.

Hinkspiel
(Hopscotch)

Playing area: Sidewalk, pavement, or hard, flat ground
Number of players: Two or more
Materials: Chalk to mark sidewalk or pavement; a flat marker for each player

This is only one type of hopscotch played in Germany. The seven circles that make up the hopscotch diagram are named after the days of the week. Sometimes, players

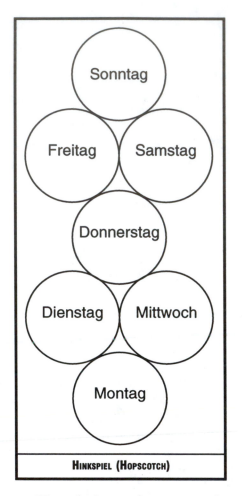

HINKSPIEL (HOPSCOTCH)

agree to make *Donnerstag* (Thursday) a resting space, where they can stand on two feet for a short while. A player begins by standing at the lower edge of the first circle and dropping or sliding her stone into *Montag* (Monday). Then she hops into that circle, kicks the stone into *Dienstag*, hops into that circle, kicks the stone into *Mittwoch,* and so on, hopping out after *Sonntag.* The sequence of the days of the week in German is:

Montag	Monday
Dienstag	Tuesday
Mittwoch	Wednesday
Donnerstag	Thursday
Freitag	Friday
Samstag	Saturday
Sonntag	Sunday

A player loses her turn to the next player if she lets her foot touch the ground, steps on a line, or fails to toss or kick the marker into the correct circle (the marker must not touch a line). When a player successfully completes one round, she stands outside the first circle with her back to the hopscotch and throws her marker over her shoulder. If the stone lands in one of the circles, she writes her name in that circle, which becomes her "house." From then on she may rest on both feet in that circle, but no other player may jump into it without her permission. After tossing the marker over her shoulder, the player begins a new round, played exactly like the first. The game ends when so many circles are owned that no player can hop the *Hinkspiel*. The winner is the player who owns the most houses.

For more information about hopscotch and a list of other hopscotch games in this book, see page 25.

Ghana
Achi

Playing area: Anywhere

Number of players: Two

Materials: A piece of paper or other flat surface on which to draw the playing diagram; four small markers for each player

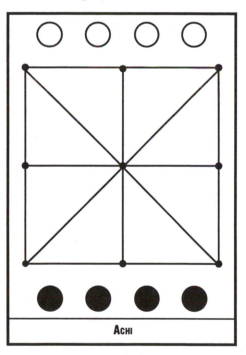

ACHI

The board is empty as the game begins. Players take turns placing one marker at a time on the board on one of the points where the lines intersect. When all eight markers have been placed, players take turns moving any one of their markers along a line to any empty point. The winner of the game is the first to get three pieces in a row.

For more information about board games and a list of other board games in this book, see page 14.

Snake Tag

Playing area: A medium-sized space, indoors or outdoors

Number of players: Two equal teams of five or more each

Materials: Two scarves or other squares of cloth

Members of each team hold onto the waist, shoulders, or clothing of the player in front, forming a snake. The last player in line tucks a scarf into her belt or back pocket. The heads of the two snakes face each other, and at a signal, each leader tries to capture the scarf of the last player on the other team's snake. If either snake breaks apart, the game must begin again.

For more information about tag and chasing games and a list of other tag and chasing games in this book, see page 37.

Greece (Ancient)
Brazen Fly

Playing area: A medium-sized, clear space, indoors or outdoors

Number of players: Six or more

Materials: None

This is the oldest recorded Blind Man's Bluff game. It was described this way by the Roman author Pollux:

> The eyes of a boy having been bound with a bandage, he goes round, saying, "I shall chase the brazen fly." But the others answer, "You will chase him but not catch him," and they hit him with whips of papyrus until he catches one of them.

The players made a buzzing sound as they tried to escape.

For more information about blindfold games and a list of other blindfold games in this book, see page 13.

Greece (Modern)
Kukla

Playing area: A clear space, indoors or outdoors, about twenty feet square

Number of players: Five or more

Materials: An empty can, such as a soup can; a beanbag for each player; chalk, if playing on pavement

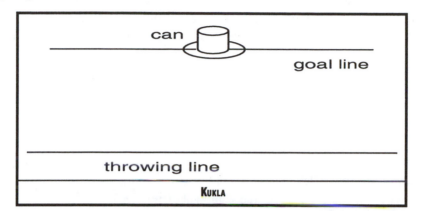

Players draw two parallel lines, about 10 feet long and 10 feet apart. One is the goal line, and the other is the throwing line. They place the can in the middle of the goal line and draw a circle, about 12 inches in diameter, around it. The players line up on the throwing line and toss their bags toward the goal line. The player whose bag lands closest to the goal line will be the first guard, and she takes a position behind the can. The other players line up behind the throwing line and, one at a time, toss their beanbags and try to hit the can and knock it onto its side. As soon as the can has been knocked down, the player who hit it must run and pick up his beanbag, then return to the throwing line. After replacing the can in the circle, the guard tries to tag that player before she gets to the throwing line. If the guard succeeds, that player becomes the new guard, and the guard joins the other throwers.

If a player or series of players fails to knock down the can, their bags must remain on the ground until someone upsets the can. Once this happens, all players must rush to retrieve their bags, avoiding the guard, who is free to try to tag any of them. The first player that is tagged by the guard becomes the guard in the next game.

For more information about tag and chasing games and a list of other tag and chasing games in this book, see page 37.

Guatemala
Wall Bounce

Playing area: A good ball-bouncing wall
Number of players: Two or more

Materials: A tennis ball or other bouncy rubber ball about the same size, for each player

Players line up about six feet away from the wall. Together they bounce their balls against the wall and catch them while saying the following chant and performing the motions indicated by the words. Anyone who makes a mistake must drop out of the game.

Sin moverse—Without moving

Sin reirme—Without laughing

Sin hablar—Without talking

En un pie—On one foot

En una mano—In one hand

Adelante—In front (Clap your hands before catching the ball)

Atrás—Behind (Clap hands behind your back before catching the ball)

Torbellino—Whirlwind (Whirl your hands before catching the ball)

Caballete—Little horse (Clap hands under one knee before catching the ball)

Ahora si—Right now! (Hold arms out straight in front of you, then catch the ball)

Media vuelta—Half turn (Turn halfway around and back, then catch the ball)

Vuelta entero—Full turn (Spin all the way around, then catch the ball)

A game very much like this is played on the sidewalks of the United States, where it is called Russia, Mamsy, Wall Ball, or Seven Up. The different ways of throwing the ball are often called "onesies," "twosies," "threesies," and so on. Players perform the motions of onesies once, those of twosies twice, threesies three times, and so on.

For more information about ball games and a list of other ball games in this book, see page 12.

Sand Game

Playing area: The seashore or other very sandy place (the sand must be wet enough so that it can be formed into solid mounds about two feet high)

Number of players: Ten or more

Materials: None

Players stand in a circle, 18 inches to two feet apart, marking their place in the sand. Then each player builds a mound at that spot, about two feet high. Players sit on the mounds. At a signal, each player raises himself up with his hands, legs extended, and pushes himself toward the mound to his left. The objective is to get to the next mound without touching feet or legs on the ground. Players move around the circle,

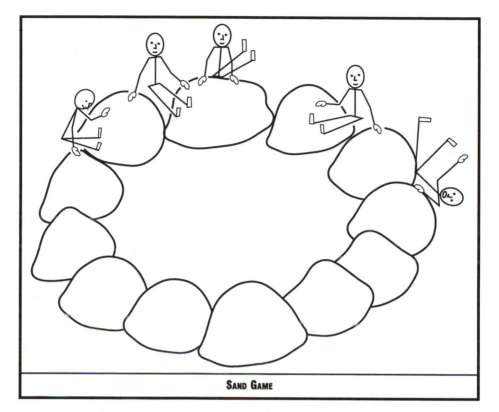

SAND GAME

and any player who does not land on the next mound or who touches the ground is out of the game.

Guyana
Ring on a String

Playing area: A space, indoors or outdoors, where players can sit comfortably on the floor or ground

Number of players: Ten to twenty

Materials: A string or thin rope just long enough to make a circle through the players' lifted hands; a ring that can slide easily over the string, yet is small enough to be easily concealed in a player's fist

Thread the string through the ring and tie the ends together. Players choose one person to be It, then sit in a circle on the ground with both arms raised in front of them, hands clasped loosely over the string. It sits in the center of the circle with eyes closed as the ring is passed along the string to one player, who conceals it in one fist. It then opens her eyes, and the players bring their hands together until they touch, then apart until they touch the hands of their neighbors, usually singing a slow rhythmic song as they play. Slyly they pass the ring along the string. The player who has the ring pretends he does not; those who do not have the ring may pretend they do. Usually the ring moves in one direction only, but good players can make it change directions, too. It watches and tries to guess who has the ring. In some games, It grabs the hand he thinks holds the ring as soon as he is sure where it is. In others, It guesses the name of the player who has the ring when the song ends. If It guesses correctly, the person with the ring takes his place. If It guesses incorrectly, he must keep his place for the next game.

Versions of this game are played in many countries, including Belgium, Denmark, England, Germany, Greece, Hungary, Indonesia, the Netherlands, Sudan, Sweden, Switzerland, and the United States. In Haiti, it is the knot tying the ends of the string together that is passed around from player to player.

Players who are new to this game will need lots of time to practice passing the ring. You may also want to limit It to three incorrect guesses before a new player takes a turn at the center of the circle.

For more information about hide-and-seek games and a list of other passing an object games in this book, see page 24.

Haiti
Marelles
(Hopscotch)

Playing area: Sidewalk, pavement, or hard, flat ground

Number of players: Two or more

Materials: Chalk to mark diagram (see page 81) on sidewalk or pavement; a flat marker for each player

Players mark playing area as shown in illustration. A player must remain silent throughout his turn. He throws his stone into the first circle, then hops into that circle, bends down, and picks up the stone. He hops into the next two circles, and when he reaches the squares, he lands on both feet, one foot in each of the first two squares, then hops on one foot into each of the second two squares. He then lands with one foot in each of the first two squares as before, then hops in each of the three circles, and hops out. The player then throws his stone into the second circle and makes a second round as before. He loses his turn if his foot or his stone touch a line, if his lifted foot touches the ground, or if he speaks or makes a sound during his turn.

For more information about hopscotch and a list of other hopscotch games in this book, see page 25.

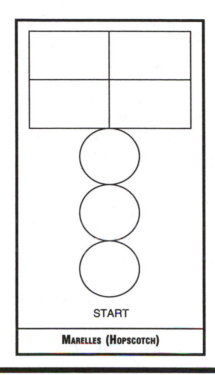

MARELLES (HOPSCOTCH)

Honduras
La Rayuela

Playing area: Sidewalk, pavement, or hard, flat ground

Number of players: Two or more

Materials: Chalk to mark sidewalk or pavement; a flat marker for each player

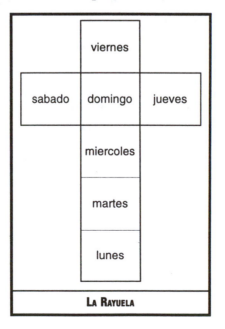

LA RAYUELA

Rayuela is Spanish for hopscotch. Players mark this hopscotch diagram on the playing surface, then hop around it in the order of the days of the week. They do best if they choose a marker that is easy to kick. In Honduras, a broken piece of pottery roof tile is often used. The first player slides her marker along the ground into *Lunes,* hops into that square, turns and kicks the marker out, and hops out. She then slides the marker into *Martes,* hops into *Lunes,* then hops into *Martes,* then kicks the marker into *Lunes,* hops into *Lunes,* kicks the marker out, and hops out, and so on for seven rounds. The first player to successfully complete the seventh round through all the days is the winner. Meanwhile, any player who touches a line or her lifted foot to the ground, or whose marker touches a line, or who slides her marker into the wrong square, loses a turn. On her next turn, she begins again on the day of the week on which she made the mistake.

For more information about hopscotch and a list of other hopscotch games in this book, see page 25.

Hungary
Dobi-dobi

Playing area: A small, clear space, indoors or outdoors

Number of players: Four or more

Materials: None

One player is chosen to be It, and he hides his face in his hands as the others join hands and form a circle around him. One player leaves the circle and stands behind It. The players begin to sing a song, and the person behind It taps It's back with the fingers of one hand, in order, to the rhythm of the song. When the song ends, It must guess which finger is on his back.

For more information about guessing games and a list of other Who Was It? games in this book, see page 20.

Iceland
Fox and Geese

Playing area: Anywhere

Number of players: Two

Materials: A piece of paper or other flat surface on which to draw the game board; thirteen markers representing the geese; one marker representing the fox

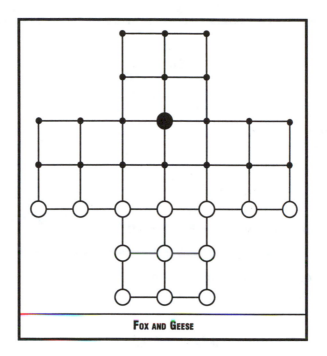

FOX AND GEESE

The moves for Fox and Geese are much like those of kings in checkers except that the markers do not rest within squares, but at the intersections of the lines on the game board.

One player places the 13 markers representing the geese on the board as in the diagram. The other player places the marker representing the fox on any vacant point.

The fox has the first move; after that, the two players take turns moving their markers in any direction along a line to the next adjacent point. The fox may jump over any goose, but it must be able to land on an empty point beyond. The goose that the fox jumped over had been "huffed" and is removed from the board. Two or more geese can be huffed by the fox in a series of short jumps, as in checkers.

The geese may not jump over the fox; they can win the game only by trapping the fox in a corner, making it impossible for him to move.

If the fox is unable to move he loses the game, but if the fox huffs enough geese to make it impossible for them to trap him, the fox wins. If the geese are played correctly, they will always win.

The earliest known reference to this game is a mention of *Hala-tafl,* "the fox game," in *Grettis Saga,* a work from Iceland written in about A.D. 1300.

For more information about board games and a list of other board games in this book, see page 14.

India
Magic Tag

Playing area: A large outdoor space

Number of players: Four or more

Materials: None

One player is chosen to be It. It announces that either stone, iron, or wood will have magic powers during the game. A player touching anything made of the magic substance cannot be tagged. It is considered bad sportsmanship for a player to touch a magic substance for too long, and sometimes players make rules about how long a person can touch the magic substance and how many times.

For more information about tag and chasing games and a list of other tag and chasing games in this book, see page 37.

Sota-pani

Playing area: A clear space, indoors or outdoors

Number of players: Ten or more

Materials: A handkerchief or scarf with a a knot tied in one corner

One player is chosen to be It. The others sit or squat, evenly spaced, in a circle. It carries the handkerchief—the *sota*—and runs around the circle of players. The players may not turn their heads to watch, but must look straight ahead. Players must use clues to discover if the handkerchief has been dropped behind them. For instance, they can watch the eyes and facial expressions of the players seated across from them, who *can* see what It is doing. The player who is It tries all sorts of tricks to confuse the other players. After a few circles, he drops the *sota* behind one of them, and that player picks up the *sota* and chases It, trying to hit him with the knotted end. The two race around the circle once, and It tries to beat the player to his seat. If It reaches the empty space in the circle first, the other player must become It in his place.

If a player does not notice that the *sota* has been dropped behind her before It completes another full circle, It picks up the handkerchief and hits the player on the back with the knot several times. That player then becomes It.

For more information about tag and chasing games and a list of other Drop the Handkerchief games in this book, see page 34.

Vultures and Crows

Playing area: Anywhere

Number of players: Two

Materials: A piece of paper or other flat surface on which the game board can be drawn; one marker for the vulture; six different-colored markers for the crows

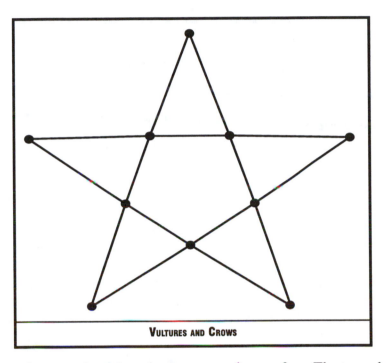

VULTURES AND CROWS

Players draw the game board on the paper or other surface. The two players have an unequal number of markers: the game pits one vulture against six crows. The vulture may jump one or more crows at a time and take them off the board. The crows may only move one space at a time. The vulture's goal is to eat all the crows (remove them from the board). The objective of the crows is to force the vulture into a corner so that it cannot move. Players may want to experiment with using five and seven crows, to see how this changes the play of the game.

To play, the player with the crows takes the first turn, placing one crow on any point on the board. Then the player with the vulture places it on any point on the board. Next turn another crow is placed. The vulture begins to move one space on every turn. It may jump over a crow, so long as it can land on an empty point beyond. That crow is then removed from the board. The vulture may eat more than one crow in a series of jumps. Meanwhile, the other player continues to place the crows until all are on the board.

Play continues with alternate moves by each player. The vulture wins if it succeeds in eating all the crows. The crows win if they can trap the vulture in a corner and prevent it from moving.

For more information about board games and a list of other board games in this book, see page 14.

Indonesia
Man, Ant, Elephant

Playing area: Anywhere

Number of players: Two

Materials: None

This game is played much like Scissors-Paper-Stone and is often used to settle arguments or to decide who will go first in a game. Players each raise one arm, bend the elbow, and swing the hand back toward the shoulder three times, counting "One, two, three." On "four," they bring their hands down in front of them in one of three signs: Thumb out is elephant; first finger out is man; little finger out is ant. The way one sign defeats another is as follows: the elephant defeats the man because he is stronger; the man defeats the ant because he is stronger; the ant defeats the elephant because the ant can run up the elephant's trunk and bite him until he goes crazy. If each player makes the same sign, they play again.

For more information about guessing games and a list of other gesture anticipation games in this book, see page 21.

Sorok-sorok

Playing area: Any space, indoors or outdoors, that offers a variety of good hiding places for the players

Number of players: Five to fifteen

Materials: A blindfold

This is a hide-and-seek game that can be played indoors as well as outdoors. One player is chosen to be It, and another is chosen to be the mother. It covers her eyes or is blindfolded while the other players (except the mother) hide. When everyone has hidden, the mother names each hidden player and asks It where he thinks that player is hiding. The first player whose hiding place is guessed must become It for a new game. If It does not guess any of the hiding places correctly, he is It for the next game.

For more information about hide-and-seek games and a list of other hide-and-seek games in this book, see page 23.

Iran
Borkum Topa
(Kick the Hat)

Playing area: A medium-sized, clear space, outdoors

Number of players: Four or more

Materials: A hat or other small, soft item of clothing for each player; chalk to mark a circle

One player is chosen to be It, and the players draw a circle, about three feet in diameter, on the ground. It tosses her hat into the ring, then stands, always with one foot on the circle line, and guards the hat from the other players, who try to steal it. It may not move the foot that is on the line, but may use the other foot to pivot around.

The other players come up to the ring and try to kick the hat out without being tagged by It. They may not use their hands. If they are tagged, they are out of the game. Once the hat has been kicked out of the ring, any player can grab it with his hands, including It. If another player grabs the hat, the only way that It can get it back is to chase and tag the player who kicked it out of the ring.

In *When I Was a Boy in Persia,* Youel Mirza wrote that when he played this game as a boy, hats were prized possessions. This made the game all the more exciting, for the players risked having their precious hats damaged and getting in trouble with their parents.

For more information about tag and chasing games and a list of other guarding the treasure games in this book, see page 36.

*Who Was It?

Playing area: A medium-sized, clear space, indoors or outdoors

Number of players: Five or more

Materials: A large, flat stone; a smaller stone

One of the players is It and plays the part of a cat, while the others are mice. The cat sits down and is blindfolded or covers her eyes. The mice line up behind her. A large, flat stone lies on the ground between cat and mice, with a little stone on top. One of the mice comes forward and taps the little stone on the big stone, as the other mice say, "Little mouse, little mouse, watch out, the cat may get you."

The mouse runs back to the other players, who say,

"Who was it? Who was it? It wasn't I!"

The cat must guess which player tapped the stone. The game continues until the cat guesses correctly. The mouse who has been identified takes the place of the cat.

For more information about guessing games and a list of other Who Was It? games in this book, see page 21.

Iraq
Knucklebones

Playing area: A clear, flat, dirt area, about eight to ten feet across
Number of players: Two or more
Materials: Several knuckleones (or substitute walnuts) for each player

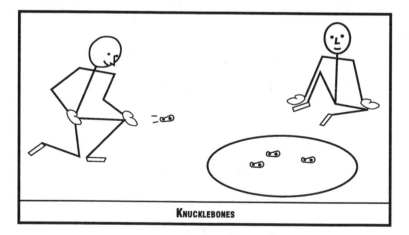

KNUCKLEBONES

Knucklebones (the small, rectangular ankle bones of cows, sheep, or goats) are used like marbles in ring games in the Mediterranean area. The bones are dyed or painted different colors so that players can identify them during a game.

In this game, players draw a circle in the dirt, then each contribute an equal number of knucklebones, placing them in or near the center of the circle. To play, each player takes a turn twirling another knucklebone, their "shooter," beginning outside the circle, and afterwards launching the shooter each time from the place where it landed. A knucklebone is twirled between the thumb and first two fingers, and propelled forward with a movement of the arm. A player gets to keep any knucklebone that his shooter knocks out of the circle.

For more information about dice, knucklebones, and games of chance, see page 17. For more information on marbles and a list of other marbles games in this book, see page 29.

For more information about dice, knucklebones, and games of chance, see page 17. For more information on marbles and a list of other marbles games in this book, see page 29.

Ireland

Pass the Brogue

Playing area: A space where players can sit on the floor or ground

Number of players: Eight or more

Materials: A pile of straw; a brogue (shoe)

One player is chosen to be It. The other players sit in a circle on the floor, knees up, with straw piled up on their legs. They begin to pass a brogue from person t o person under their knees while saying, "Pass the brogue around, pass it, pass it." All pretend to pass the shoe, while really they might not have it. One player may have it and be holding onto it. The leader keeps guessing who has the brogue until she is successful.

The person who is holding the shoe when it is found bends forward while another player beats on her back saying, "Hurly burly, thump on the back, how many horns do I hold up?" Then the thumper holds up one or more fingers, and the bent-over player must guess how many there are. If she fails to guess correctly, an object is placed on her back as the others chant, "Heavy, heavy, what is on your back?"

If she fails to identify the object on her back, more and more objects are piled on top, until one is guessed. Then that player becomes It for the next round of the game.

In games like this from other countries, the players may pass the shoe (or other object) behind their backs. In Algeria, children sit with their knees up and pass a stone around the circle under their long robes.

For more information about hide-and-seek games and a list of other passing an object games in this book, see page 24.

For more information about hide-and-seek games and a list of other passing an object games in this book, see page 24.

Israel
Hat Race

Playing area: A large, clear outdoor space

Number of players: Ten or more

Materials: A hat for each player; a rope for each team

This is a race for two or more teams with an equal number of players. Players draw two long parallel lines, about 20 feet apart, on the ground. One line is the starting line. Players place their hats in separate piles, one for each team, on the line opposite. Then they line up opposite their hat pile on the starting line. Players must hold onto their team's rope with both hands for the entire race, so that they cannot use their hands to pick up the hats. At a signal, they run to the pile and begin putting on their hats. Teamwork is necessary, because players may *not* use their hands. The winning team is the one that arrives back at the starting point with each member wearing a hat.

For more information about racing games and a list of other racing games in this book, see page 31.

Italy
Angels and Demons

Playing area: A medium-sized, clear space, indoors or outdoors

Number of players: Ten to twenty

Materials: None

Two players are chosen to be the angel and the demon, and they decide together secretly which of them is which. They also choose two other names that they will use for themselves during the game (usually the names of colors or flowers).

The angel and the devil join hands and make an arch. The other players form a line, with hands on each others' shoulders, and pass beneath the arch as the angel and demon chant, "Go along, go along, since the last one will be mine." On the word "mine," they bring their arms down and trap a player. They ask that person to choose between the two color or flower names they have chosen, and the player whispers his choice. Then he gets behind the person he has chosen. The game continues until all the players but one have been trapped and taken sides. The last player runs back and forth underneath the arch as everyone chants the names of the days of the week, *"lunedí* (Monday), *martedí* (Tuesday), *mercoledí* (Wednesday), *giovedí* (Thursday), *venerdí* (Friday), *sabato* (Saturday)." On *"domenica"* (Sunday), the last player is trapped also.

Finally, the angel and demon reveal their secret identities. Those players who chose the side of the demon are laughed at and sometimes made to pay forfeits. (See Forfeits, page 19.)

For more information about London Bridge games and a list of other London Bridge games in this book, see page 28.

Morra

Playing area: Anywhere
Number of players: Two
Materials: None

Players decide beforehand how many points make up a game (usually five or 10 points). In unison, the players count to three while moving their right fists up and down, like hammers. Then each player puts out from one to five fingers and, at precisely the same instant, calls out a number from two to 10. This is their guess at the total number of fingers they have both held out. Many times neither player will guess correctly. Players score a point for each correct guess.

Players of this game are depicted on Egyptian monuments erected nearly 4,000 years ago. They are shown playing with the fingers of the right hand and keeping score with those of the left, very much as players in Italy do today. To keep score of up to 12 on the fingers of one hand, use the thumb to touch the first joint of each finger, beginning with the forefinger, then the second joint of each finger, then the tips.

For more information about memory games and a list of other number and counting games in this book, see page 30. For more information about guessing games and a list of other gesture anticipation games in this book, see page 21.

*Wolf and Lamb

Playing area: A medium-sized space, indoors or outdoors
Number of players: Ten or more
Materials: None

Players hold hands and form a circle. One is chosen as the lamb and stands inside the circle, and another is the wolf and stands outside. They say:

Lamb: I am the lamb.
Wolf: I am the wolf, and I am going to catch you!
Lamb: Oh no, you won't!

The wolf tries to catch the lamb, and the players in the circle try to help the lamb stay away. Both lamb and wolf may go inside or outside the circle, and the players may raise or lower their arms to help the lamb or stop the wolf. When the lamb is caught, that player joins the circle, the wolf becomes the lamb, and another player becomes the wolf.

For more information about tag and chasing games and a list of other cat-and-mouse games in this book, see page 34.

For more information about tag and chasing games and a list of other cat-and-mouse games in this book, see page 34.

Ivory Coast

Awele

Playing area: Anywhere

Number of players: Two

Materials: An *awele* game board, or a piece of paper or other flat surface on which to draw the game; forty-eight small markers, such as dried peas, beans, small shells, or tiny rocks

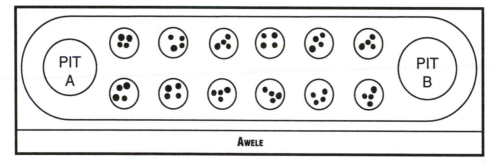

AWELE

The best boards for mancala games like this one are carved from wood, but a game board can just as easily be drawn on paper or another flat surface. (Players will need to be careful not to scatter the markers by mistake.) An *Awele* game board looks very much like an egg carton, but its depressions are much shallower. It is difficult for adults or children to reach or see into the depressions of an egg carton, so this item really cannot be used to play the game. Game boards can easily be made from self-hardening clay, or a playing area may be scooped in moist sand.

To set up the game, each player puts four markers in every hole on her side of the board, but not in the scoring pits at the ends of the boards.

To play, each player, in turn, scoops up all the counters from any one hole on her side of the board. She then moves her hand counterclockwise around the board, placing or "sowing" one marker in each hole until there are no more markers in her hand. A player can capture markers from her opponent's side of the board whenever the last seed sown lands in a hole on that side that holds either one or two markers. If the next-to-last hole contains just one or two markers, the player wins those also. When a player captures an opponent's markers, she removes all the markers in the hole and puts them in her scoring pit. Markers may not be captured from a hole if the move takes away the only counters left on an opponent's side.

The game is over when neither player can get around to the opposite side of the board. The player who made the last capture collects any markers that remain on the board. The winner is the player with the most captured markers.

Awele is just one version of an African board game, part of the family of mancala games. The same game is called *Wari* in Senegal, Gambia, Guinea, Ghana, and in African American communities in North and South America. In Sierra Leone it is called *Kboo*; in Nigeria, *Ayoayo;* and in Cameroon, *Ayo.* The earliest known Mancala board was found in Egypt: a game board was cut into a stone at the temple of Kurna, which was built around 1400 B.C.

Today, games of this type are played in many parts of Africa by both adults and children. The game is easy to set up—scoop holes in the sand, find some counters, and challenge a friend to a game.

For more information about board games and a list of other board games in this book, see page 14.

Jamaica
Because, Yes, and No

Playing area: Indoors or outdoors

Number of players: Five or more

Materials: None

Two players are chosen to play the roles of master and banker. The master goes around and asks the players questions that the players must answer fully and truthfully, but they may not use the words "Yes," "No," or "Because." The master can ask a player one question or several related questions. If a player uses a forbidden word, he must give something he owns to the banker, and after a certain number of questions or a certain period of time, which the players have decided beforehand, players can retrieve their possessions from the banker by paying forfeits. (See Forfeits, page 19.)

For more information about storytelling and word games and a list of other storytelling and word games in this book, see page 33.

Japan
Fuku Wari

Playing area: An indoor or outdoor area near a wall

Number of players: Three or more

Materials: A large sheet of paper; crayons or markers; masking tape

Oni Face. Draw it without the features, then cut them separately from construction paper.

FUKU WARI

Fuku Wari is a festival and party game, like Pin the Tail on the Donkey. A face without features is drawn on a large sheet of paper, and the paper is taped to a wall. When the game is played during New Year celebrations in Japan, the face of *Otafuku*, the goddess of fortune, is drawn. At other times, the face of an *oni*—a Japanese giant or ogre—is used. *Onis* are said to have red or green faces, with sharp horns on their foreheads.

Draw a blank *oni* face on a large piece of paper and attach it to the wall. Use construction paper to draw and cut out scary eyes and a nose and mouth for your *oni*. Stick a loop of masking tape on the back of each one.

The players take turns being blindfolded. Each stands in front of the *oni* face and is given the eyes, nose, and mouth, one by one, to place on it. You can give a prize for the most correct *oni* face, but the real fun of the game is laughing at the

9 4

silly, mixed-up monster faces the children make. This is a good game for older children to organize for younger ones.

Jan Ken Po

Playing area: Anywhere

Number of players: See instructions below for number of players needed for the two different versions of this game

Materials: None

Jan Ken Po is very much like Scissors-Paper-Stone, a game played in the United States. *Jan Ken Po* can be played by a group of three or more, with one person taking the role of "changer." The changer pounds his fist three times, saying *"jan ken po,"* and on *po,* he makes one of three signs with his hand: a hand opened flat, palm down, is paper; a hand closed in a fist except for first and second fingers spread in a "V," represents scissors; and a closed fist is stone. When the changer makes paper, scissors, or stone, the others must immediately make the thing that defeats that object: scissors defeats (cuts) paper, stone defeats (breaks) scissors, and paper defeats (wraps) stone. Anyone making the wrong gesture is out of the game, and play continues until one player is left. That player becomes the new changer.

In Japan, *Jan Ken Po* is often used to decide who will be It in a game. *Jan Ken Po* is also played by two people in the same way that Scissors-Paper-Stone is played in the United States. For a variation of this type of game that does not use scissors, paper, and stone, see Indonesia: Man, Ant, Elephant.

For more information about guessing games and a list of other gesture anticipation games in this book, see page 21.

Otedama

Playing area: A flat, clear space on floor, dirt, or pavement

Number of players: Two or more

Materials: Seven tiny cloth bags, about an inch square, filled with rice

One bag is the taw, and players toss it in the air. The taw is usually flat, while the others are gathered up a bit so that they are more rounded. The taw may be a different color than the others.

These tiny beanbag jacks make for a different type of play than that performed with stones, metal jacks, seeds, or shells. Many complicated series of moves are performed with these jacks. The following are just a few:

- A player tosses the taw up and picks up the other bags one at a time, catching the taw before it hits the ground. He tosses the taw again, then picks up the bags two at a time, and so on to six. He picks up odd numbers of leftover bags as a group. Then he tosses up the taw and catches it on the back of his hand, then tosses it up from there and catches it with the fingertips of the same hand, without turning the hand over.

- The player scatters the six bags slightly. She tosses up the taw, then grabs all six bags and catches the taw in her palm along with them. She tosses up the taw again, then slaps the six bags to the floor so that the taw falls onto the back of her hand and stays there.

- The player places all seven bags in a row on the floor, with the taw to the right of them. Beginning with the bag to the far left, he picks up each bag with the thumb and forefinger, the palm facing down. Then he tosses the bag and catches it on the back of his hand. The first bag remains there as he picks up the second bag, but he tosses it off before he catches the second bag. This play continues until the taw has been successfully tossed and caught.

For more information about jacks games and a list of other jacks games in this book, see page 26.

Jordan
Tied-up Monkey

Playing area: Outdoors, around a tree trunk or post
Number of players: Five or more
Materials: A piece of rope about twelve feet long

TIED-UP MONKEY

Players draw a circle, about three or four feet in diameter, around the base of the tree or post. They tie the rope to the tree or post, leaving a free end about nine feet long. They choose one player to be the monkey, and he must hold onto the end of the rope at all times. Each of the other players puts one or both shoes inside the circle. As the game begins, the players try to retrieve their shoes without being tagged by the monkey. A player tagged by the monkey takes the monkey's place.

In a version of this game from Algeria, It plays the role of a camel and must hold the rope between his teeth and walk on all fours as he tries to tag the others.

For more information about tag and chasing games and a list of other guarding the treasure games in this book, see page 36.

Kenya
Jackstones

Playing area: A flat, clear space on floor, dirt, or pavement

Number of players: Three or more

Materials: Ten to fifteen palm nuts (or substitute peach or plum pits or unshelled almonds) for each player

Players sit in a circle on the ground and place all their palm nuts in a pile at the center. Each player keeps one nut to toss into the air. He tosses the nut and, before it comes down, scoops up as many nuts as he can from the pile, catching the falling nut with the same hand. Then it is the next player's turn, and so on, until all nuts are taken. The player who has the most nuts at the end of the game is the winner. A player who misses the falling nut must put the nuts she just took back in the pile.

For more information about jacks games and a list of other jacks games in this book, see page 26.

Korea
Marbles

Playing area: A medium-sized, flat, dirt area

Number of players: Four to eight

Materials: An equal number of marbles for each player

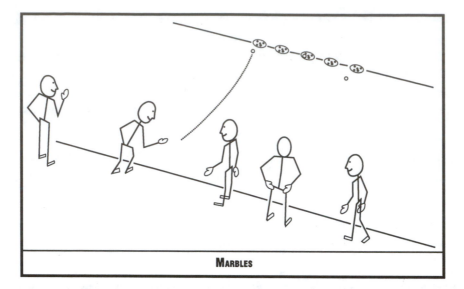

MARBLES

Players draw two parallel lines on the ground, about 15 feet apart. All of the players dig individual holes (one per player), about three inches across, on one of the lines. There must not be a lip at the edge of the holes, because this will prevent marbles from rolling into them. Each player owns the hole he has dug and marks it in some special way.

One player is chosen to roll first. That player stands on the throwing line and rolls a marble, trying to get it into her own hole. If it should go into another player's hole, that player must go pick up the marble, then run and tag the thrower. If he succeeds in tagging her, he keeps the marble. Sometimes this game is played for keeps, and sometimes the marbles are returned to their owners at the end of the game, along with a rap on the hand.

For more information about marbles and a list of other marbles games in this book, see page 29.

*Mek Konk

Playing area: A small space, indoors or outdoors

Number of players: Six to twelve

Materials: An equal number of small objects, such as pine nuts (traditional), pebbles, or beans, in a sack or pocket for each player (each player needs three objects for each player in the game)

The players form a line, and the player at the head of the line is the first challenger. The challenger secretly places several nuts in one hand (as many as he wishes to wager), then holds both hands out toward the second player, who must guess which hand holds the nuts. If she guesses correctly, she wins the nuts. If she is wrong, she must hand over the same number of nuts that the challenger has in his hand. The first player continues, challenging each player in line, then takes his place at the end of the line, and the second player becomes the challenger. When every player has had a turn being the challenger, the player with the most nuts wins.

In the United States, children play a similar game, called Hul Gul, with grains of corn, and games very much like this are found in England, Germany, Ireland, Italy, and Japan.

For more information about guessing games and a list of other Who Has It? games in this book, see page 21.

Laos
Jack Sticks

Playing area: A flat, clear space on floor, dirt, or pavement

Number of players: Two or more

Materials: Fifteen or more sticks, eight or ten inches long, such as small chopsticks or pick-up sticks; a round nut or small ball, like a jacks ball

To decide who plays first, each player in turn takes the sticks in his or her hand, tosses them up, and tries to catch as many as possible on the back of the hand. The player who catches the most begins the game by scattering the sticks on the ground. He tosses the ball up, picks up one stick, and catches the ball before it touches the ground. If he misses the ball or fails to pick up a stick, the next player takes a turn. The player who picks up the most sticks is the winner.

In a more challenging version of this game, a player must pick up one stick on the first toss, two on the second, and so on.

For more information about jacks games and a list of other jacks games in this book, see page 26.

Latvia
Horns, Horns, Who Has Horns?

Playing area: Table and chairs

Number of players: Four or more

Materials: None

The players sit around a table. One is chosen as the leader. He knocks on the table as he says, "Horns, horns, horns," and the other players do the same. Then the leader names an animal, such as a deer, saying, "Deers have horns." The others immediately raise one hand to their foreheads, with their forefinger and middle finger extended in the form of horns, as they repeat the leader's words, "Deers have horns." They do this *only* if the animal has horns. If a player makes horns for an animal that does not have horns, such as a pig, or fails to make horns for an animal that does have them, she is out of the game. The last player left in the game becomes the new leader. This game is played very quickly and rhythmically.

This game has also been recorded in Denmark, Finland, Greece, Norway, Sweden, and the United States.

For more information about category games and a list of other category games in this book, see page 15.

Lebanon
Do You Have Fire?

Playing area: A clear square or rectangular area, fifteen feet or so on a side
Number of players: Five
Materials: None

Players mark the playing area so that it is easy to see the corners. Or players may choose four objects, such as trees, as corners. One player is selected as It, and each of the others goes to a corner. It approaches one player (going close enough that their hands could touch), asking, "Neighbor, do you have fire?" The player answers, "No, my neighbor has fire." While It is questioning one player, any two of the others try to change places. It tries to tag one of them, but cannot begin the chase until the person he is questioning has finished her answer. If he succeeds in tagging a runner, the runner becomes It. It may not tag a player who is touching a corner base.

A similar game, Pussy Wants a Corner, is played in England and the United States. In this game, It must get to an empty base before another player, rather than tag a runner.

For more information about tag and chasing games and a list of other exchanging places games in this book, see page 36.

Liberia
Jumping Game

Playing area: A medium-sized, clear space, indoors or outdoors
Number of players: Fifteen to thirty
Materials: None

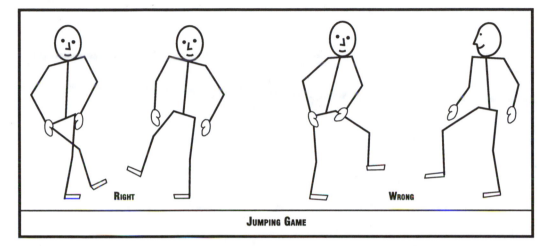

RIGHT WRONG

JUMPING GAME

One player is chosen as It. The others form a circle around her and clap their hands to the rhythm of a song, or simply clap together. It is important to establish a strong, even rhythm. It stands with her hands on her hips. To the rhythm of the clapping, she hops or jumps toward one of the other players, stands directly in front of him, then suddenly lifts one leg toward that player, toe pointing down. That player must immediately lift the same foot (right or left). The feet are opposite and will not touch. But if the player lifts the wrong foot (mirroring It) or fails to lift a foot at exactly the same time that It does, that player must take It's place in the center of the circle.

For more information about guessing games and a list of other gesture anticipation games in this book, see page 21.

Libya
Hop Tag

Playing area: A clear space, indoors or outdoors
Number of players: Six or more
Materials: None

One player is chosen to be It, and the rest stand in a line. It signals that he is about to begin chasing them by shouting *"Taia-ya-taia!"* He must chase them while hopping on one foot. The other players try to touch him, and he tries to tag them. If he succeeds in tagging another player without putting down his foot, the tagged player must take his place.

In this type of traditional tag game, the players do not simply try to "win" by not being tagged. They tempt fate by coming as close to being tagged as they can.

For more information about tag and chasing games and a list of other tag and chasing games in this book, see page 37.

Luxembourg
Hoop Game

Playing area: A good ball-bouncing wall next to an open area

Number of players: Ten to thirty

Materials: A small- to medium-sized ball, very soft and without much bounce

HOOP GAME

Players all stand about 10 feet back from the wall, and one of them throws the ball at the wall and calls the name of another player. All the players except the one whose name was called run away. The player whose name was called catches the ball as quickly as she can and calls, "Stop!" Then all the players turn their backs to that player and hold their hands over their heads in a hoop shape. The player with the ball may take up to three steps toward any player, then she throws the ball gently through the hoop formed by that player's arms. If she succeeds, the player through whose arms she threw the ball gets one penalty point and becomes the thrower for the next round. If the thrower fails to get the ball through the hoop, she takes a penalty point and throws the ball to start the next round. The player with the fewest penalty points at the end of the game is the winner.

For more information about ball games and a list of other ball games in this book, see page 12.

Malawi
Chuchu

Playing area: The game diagram is traditionally marked on dirt or sand, but it may also be marked with chalk on a sidewalk or on paper

Number of players: Ten or more, divided into two equal teams

Materials: Three stones of different colors

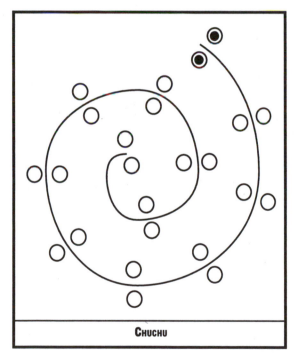

CHUCHU

A spiral is drawn in the sand, with pairs of holes marked along it on either side. Players vary the number of holes according to how long they want the game to last, but they make at least 10 pairs of holes. They put a stone in each of the outermost holes, one for each team. The team's stones advance to the center of the spiral according to their skill in guessing which member of the other team is hiding the playing stone.

One member of the first team takes the playing stone, and each player on that team puts his palms together. The leader pretends to give the stone to each, but only really gives it to one. The members of the other team decide together who has the stone. If they are correct, their stone moves forward one space on the spiral. Whether the guess is right or wrong, the right to hide the stone passes to the second team, and the first team guesses, and so on until one team's stone reaches the last hole of the spiral, and they are declared the winners.

For more information about guessing games and a list of other Who Has It? games in this book, see page 21.

Malaysia
Main China Buta

Playing area: A medium-sized space, indoors or outdoors, with good hiding places
Number of players: Three or more
Materials: A blindfold; a flute or similar instrument; a ring or ringlike bracelet

One player is chosen to be It and another to be the flute player. It is blindfolded, while another player hides the ring. It then searches for the ring, as the flute player helps her by playing lower notes as she goes further away from the ring and higher notes as she gets closer to it.

In a similar game from Ethiopia, someone signals how close the seeker is to the hidden object by playing notes on a six-stringed lyre, playing loudly when the seeker is close and softly when he is further away. In a game from Russia, one of the players hides a ring somewhere on her body, and an accordion player helps the seeker by playing louder as the seeker gets closer to the ring. In games from Europe and the Americas, players help the blindfolded seeker by saying "cold," "warm," and "hot," to indicate how close she is to the hidden object (see Paraguay: *El Pan Quemado*).

For more information about hide-and-seek and a list of other hidden object games in this book, see page 23.

Main Serembam

Playing area: A clear outdoor space

Number of players: Two or more

Materials: Ten to twenty small shells or pebbles for each player; a large bowl

The players sit in a circle, with the bowl placed in the center. Each player has the same number of small shells on the ground in front of her; 15 or 20 is the usual number. Each player puts a shell on the back of her hand and tosses it up in the air. While the shell is in the air, she takes a shell from her pile with the same hand, then catches the tossed shell on the back of her hand. Each time a player either fails to pick up a shell or misses a catch, she must put one of her shells in the bowl. The winner of the game is the last player to have two shells left.

For more information about jacks games and a list of other jacks games in this book, see page 26.

Mali

Sey

Playing area: Seashore or sandbox

Number of players: Two

Materials: A small pebble

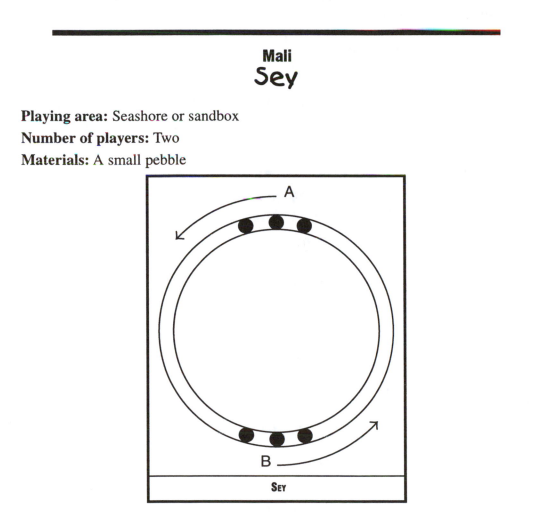

SEY

This is a guessing game for two players. Correct guesses allow them to move pebbles along a path. Players create a level playing area, about three feet square, in the sand. Then they draw a circle about two feet across, and a second circle around that one, so that they have a circular track, about an inch or two wide, between the lines.

Players sit opposite each other, and each one digs three holes, about an inch apart, right in front of himself. With the finger, players mark an equal number of dots between the two players' holes. These dots mark spots where more holes will be dug as the game progresses.

To begin the game, one player takes dry sand in his cupped hands. Concealed in his hands along with the sand is the pebble, called the *tibi*. He then lets sand fall into each of his three holes in turn. Using a thumb or finger, the player manipulates the *tibi* so that it goes into one of the holes, and he hopes that the other player does not see it. (This is more difficult than it sounds, and players should take time to practice this skill before playing the game.) The second player tries to guess which hole contains the *tibi*. If she fails to guess the correct hole, the first player digs a new hole on the spot just to the right of his three holes. Then it is his turn to hide the *tibi* again, but he may never hide it in the same hole twice; thus, he has to be careful which three holes he chooses on the next turn.

When the second player guesses correctly, it becomes her turn to hide the *tibi*. When a player's line of holes reaches his opponent's first hole, that player wins the game.

For more information about guessing games and a list of other Who Has It? games in this book, see page 21.

Mexico
Las Chivas
(Beans)

Playing area: A medium-sized, clear space, indoors or outdoors

Number of players: Four or more

Materials: Ten to twenty dried beans for each player; a wide, shallow bowl

Players place the bowl on the ground, then draw a throwing line about eight feet away (closer for younger children) from which beans are tossed into the bowl. Players begin with an equal number of beans, from 10 to 20 depending on the size of the their hands. All the beans are thrown at once. Then the player takes the beans that have landed in the hole or bowl and places them on the back of one hand. The player tosses these into the air and catches them in his palm. When all players have had a turn, the one with the most beans in his palm wins.

For more information about jacks games and a list of other jacks games in this book, see page 26.

Coin Toss

Playing area: A post, two to three feet high, that is flat on top and surrounded by flat open space

Number of players: Two or more

Materials: Five or more coins

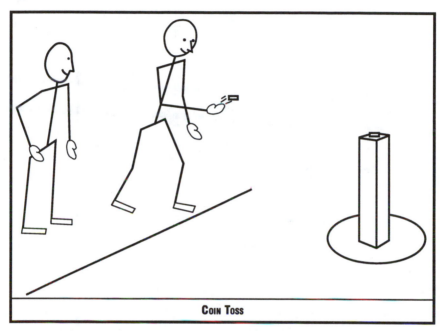

COIN TOSS

Players place a coin on the post. Then they draw a line three to six feet away and a circle, about three feet in diameter, around the base of the post. Players stand at the line and pitch coins at the coin on the post, trying to knock it off. The coin must land outside the circle for the thrower to score. This is not an easy game.

Early Spanish writers reported that official competitions of a game like this were held among Aztec warriors and that the winners were rewarded with bars of gold.

For more information about target games and a list of other target games in this book, see page 38.

Native Tarascan
El Coyote

Playing area: Anywhere

Number of players: Two

Materials: A piece of paper, board, or flat space in the dirt on which to draw the playing diagram; beans, coins, or bottle caps, one of one color to represent the coyote and twelve of another color to represent the chickens

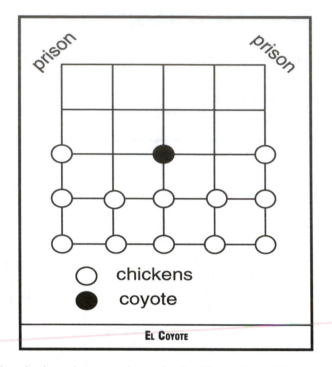

El Coyote

Players set up the playing pieces as shown in the illustration. All moves are from and to the points where the lines cross.

The coyote moves first, then the two players alternate moves. The coyote can capture, or "eat," a chicken by jumping over it, as in checkers, but it can only jump one chicken during a turn. The chickens cannot jump, but can only move one space at a time in any direction.

The coyote wins if it eats all the chickens. The chickens win if they force the coyote onto a corner, so that its only possible move will be onto one of the two prison corners.

This is a game of the Alquerque group (see Spain: *Alquerque*) and was almost certainly introduced by the Spanish.

For more information about board games and a list of other board games in this book, see page 14.

Peleche

Playing area: Sidewalk, pavement, or hard, flat ground

Number of players: Two or more

Materials: Chalk to mark sidewalk or pavement; a flat marker for each player

The players begin by marking the diagram on the playing surface. Then one player stands at the starting line and throws his marker over "Hell" and into the first box.

108

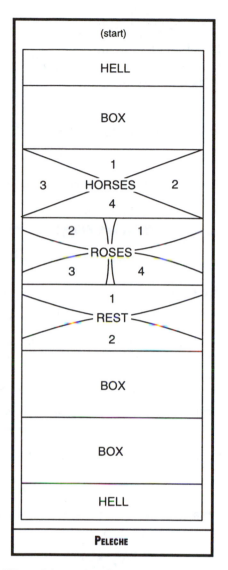

Then he hops over "Hell" and into the first box, turns around (still on one foot), places the marker on the toes of his raised foot, kicks it up and over the starting line, then hops out. A player must never put his raised foot down except in a rest square, and he must never hop in either of the two squares marked "Hell." His marker must always land in the correct square and must not touch a line. The penalty for these mistakes is to lose a turn and start again on the next turn at the same level at which he made the mistake. If the marker or a foot ever lands in "Hell," though, a player must start over from the beginning.

After completing one round, a player throws his marker into the first section of "horses," hops into the first box, then hops into the first section of "horses," turns, puts his marker on his raised foot, and kicks it out as before. The fourth section of both "horses" and "roses" are rest squares, as are both of the spaces in "rest." A player may stand on two feet and rest in any of these squares. If a player does not make a mistake, he continues this pattern of throwing, hopping, and kicking until he reaches the farthest box. Then he begins again, using the opposite end of the hopscotch as his starting line.

For more information about hopscotch and a list of other hopscotch games in this book, see page 25.

Morocco
Tabuaxrat

Playing area: A small, clear patch of ground outdoors

Number of players: Three or four

Materials: For each player, ten stones the size of hazelnuts and one smaller stone

The larger stones used for this game should be big enough so that holding two in one hand is a bit difficult. Players place all the large stones in one central pile on the ground. They sit around the pile, and one begins the game by throwing his small stone in the air. He takes one stone from the pile without disturbing any of the others. If another stone moves more than just a bit, the player must pick up that stone, too, before catching his small stone. A player who makes a mistake loses his turn.

For more information about jacks games and a list of other jacks games in this book, see page 26.

Mozambique
*Umake
(The Coast)

Playing area: A small, open space of sand or soft dirt

Number of players: Two

Materials: Three pebbles, or similar objects, of different colors

This game for two players is played on sand or dirt. With a finger or a stick, players draw a spiral, as in the diagram, on the ground. They mark resting places along the line by spreading the thumb and first finger apart and making small holes along the path that far apart. The last dot on the outer edge of the spiral, *umake,* or the coast, is the goal of the game.

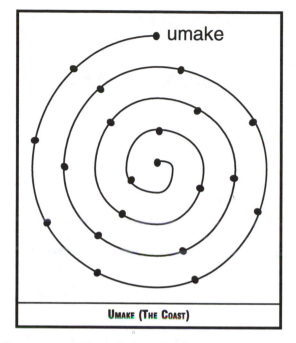

umake

UMAKE (THE COAST)

Each player chooses a pebble and places it in the center hole of the spiral. The first player takes the third pebble and moves it back and forth between her hands, then closes both fists and asks the second player to guess which one it is in. The second player taps one fist, saying *"kikote nno,"* then taps the second, saying *"kilye nno,"* then guesses which fist it is in. If she is right, she moves her pebble forward one place; if she is wrong, she does not move the pebble. Then it is the second player's turn to hide the stone, and so on. The first player to reach the coast wins the game.

For more information about guessing games and a list of other Who Has It? games in this book, see page 21.

Myanmar (Burma)
Frog Dance

Playing area: A medium-sized, clear space, indoors or outdoors

Number of players: Four or more

Materials: None

Players squat on their haunches and hop around. As they hop, they must rhythmically kick out first one foot, then the other, while clapping hands in front, then behind. Players try to make the others fall down, and the last one left upright is the winner.

For a gentler game, add a rule that players may not actually touch each other, but they can make faces and come very close, as if they were going to touch.

*Guessing Game

Playing area: A clear space, indoors or outdoors, where players can sit on the ground or the floor

Number of players: Ten or more

Materials: Two small twigs or similar objects that are easy to hide

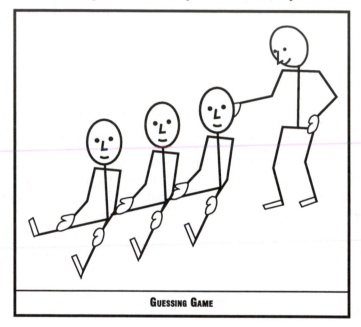

GUESSING GAME

The players are divided into two teams, each with a leader. The members of each team sit in a line, one behind another, legs straight out in front. Each leader in turn takes a small twig and walks down their team's line, pretending to place the twig under each player's leg, and actually hiding it under the legs of one player. Then each leader goes to the other team and tries to find their twig by touching each player's ears. The player with the hottest ears is supposed to be the one holding the twig. The team whose leader finds the twig with the least number of incorrect guesses is the winner of the round.

For more information on hide-and-seek games and a list of other hidden object games in this book, see page 23.

Nepal
Dhandi-biu

Playing area: A large, open, outdoor space

Number of players: Two or more

Materials: A long, flat stick; a large seed, such as a peach or plum pit

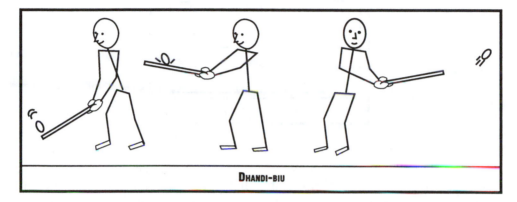

DHANDI-BIU

Players place the seed on the ground. Using the stick as a bat, a player hits the seed on one end, trying to make it flip into the air. When it does, the player must hit the seed into the air lightly twice more, then on the third hit, knock it as far as possible. The player who hits the seed farthest on his turn is the winner.

The Netherlands
Water Hopscotch

Playing area: Sidewalk, pavement, or hard, flat ground

Number of players: Two or more

Materials: Chalk to mark sidewalk or pavement; a flat marker for each player

There is extra danger in the "water" of this game. In most hopscotch games, a player loses her turn if her foot or her marker land on a line or outside the lines. If a player's foot or marker land entirely or mostly in the water area in Water Hopscotch, that player is out of the game for good! To make it a bit easier for players to avoid falling into the water, Water Hopscotch has more rest spaces than most hopscotch games. These are marked with an "R" in the diagram.

A player stands anywhere behind the base line (the line across the bottom of squares one and 10) and tosses or slides her marker into the first square. She then hops into the first square, kicks the marker back across the base line (always with the

113

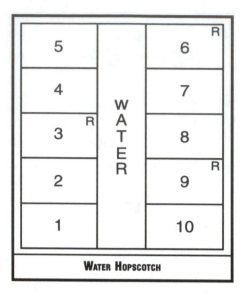

Water Hopscotch

hopping foot), and hops out. Then she tosses or slides her marker into square two, hops into square one, hops into square two, kicks the marker into square one, hops into square one, kicks the marker out, then hops out. This continues through square 10. Squares three, six, and nine are rests; that means that a player may rest there with both feet on the ground for a moment.

A player loses her turn if her lifted foot touches the ground (except in a rest square) or if her marker or her foot lands on a line or outside the desired square. On her next turn, she begins at the same level at which she missed in the previous round. If all or most of her foot or marker lands in the water area, she is out of the game. Once a player has completed round 10, she must hop the entire pattern three times on one foot, without stopping or resting, before she is declared the winner.

For more information about hopscotch and a list of other hopscotch games in this book, see page 25.

New Zealand
Folding Arms

Playing area: A large, clear, outdoor space or gymnasium

Number of players: Ten or more

Materials: A soft ball or other soft round object, such as a beanbag

One player holds the ball while all the other players stand in a line, shoulder to shoulder, with their arms folded across their chests. The player throws the ball to any player in line, and that player must quickly unfold his arms and catch it. If a player misses the ball, he is out. The player throwing the ball may also pretend she is about to throw the ball. If a player in line unfolds his arms, and the ball is not thrown to him, he is out also. The last player left in the line becomes the new thrower.

Players will need to decide what, exactly, constitutes unfolding arms; for instance, having a space between the fingertips of the two hands.

For more information about ball games and a list of other ball games in this book, see page 12.

Native Maori
Hipitoi

Playing area: Indoors or outdoors

Number of players: Two

Materials: None

This is one of many gesture-copying games, called *hakas,* of the native Maori people of New Zealand. Some of these fast-paced and competitive games are played with the arms and the whole body, but *Hipitoi* is played with the thumbs. Re-creating this game will challenge older students.

Two players face each other and present their clenched fists, thumbs up. One player begins by making one of the four gestures allowed in the game:

Both thumbs up

Left thumb up

Right thumb up

Both thumbs down (clenched)

Players alternate making a gesture first. As the first player makes the gesture he has chosen, he says "*hipitoi.*" The second player copies (mirrors) the gesture as quickly as possible, saying nothing. Then the second player says "*hipitoi*" while making a new gesture, and the first player copies it silently.

The winner of a round scores a point and a winner is decided as follows: A round ends when the copying player makes the same gesture as the lead player at exactly the same time. If the leader can then say "*ra*" before the copying player makes his new gesture and says "*hipitoi,*" the leader wins the round. If the copying player says "*hipitoi*" first, he is the winner.

For more information about guessing games and a list of other gesture anticipation games in this book, see page 21.

Nicaragua (Native American—Miskito)
Jaguar Game

Playing area: An open outdoor area

Number of players: Seven to fifteen

Materials: none

This game was played by the Miskito Indians. Similar games have been recorded among other tribes of Central and South America. One player is chosen to be the jaguar, and the others line up behind a leader, with the taller and stronger players in front. The jaguar attempts to tag the last player in line while the others try to prevent her from doing this. The jaguar must chase the other players while running on two hands and one leg, holding the other leg in the air, like the tail of a jaguar. Whenever the last player is tagged, that player leaves the game. The skill of playing the jaguar role is not easily acquired.

Games like this one, in which It is given a physical handicap, will only work when one of the stronger, faster players takes the It role. This game is tailor made for a mixed-age group.

For more information about tag and chasing games and a list of other line tag games in this book, see page 35.

Nigeria
Chiwewi

Playing area: A medium-sized, clear space, outdoors or indoors

Number of players: Five to fifteen

Materials: A rope, the length of which determines and is determined by the size of the circle formed by the players; a large beanbag or similar soft object that is tied to one end of the rope (When a player swings the rope, the beanbag on the other end should pass just below the feet of the players, who stand in a circle.)

One player is chosen to swing the rope, and he stands or squats at the center of a circle formed by the other players. He then swings the rope around, taking care that the beanbag does not rise higher than the players' knees. If the twirler stands, he will have to turn around as he swings the rope; if he squats, he can twirl it above his head. The players in the circle must jump over the beanbag. Any player whose legs touch the rope or the beanbag is out of the game, and the last player left jumping takes a turn at swinging the rope as the game begins again.

For more information about jump-rope games and a list of other jump-rope games in this book, see page 27.

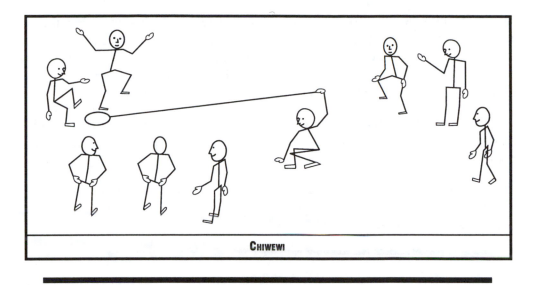

CHIWEWI

Norway
Thor's Hammer

Playing area: A medium-sized, clear area, indoors or outdoors

Number of players: Five or more

Materials: A large sheet of paper; crayons or markers; a rubber toy hammer

Thor was the name of the old Norse god of thunder, who was said to carry a hammer. The hammer was called *Mjollnir* and had magic powers. One of its powers was that it would always return to Thor's hand, like a boomerang.

This game is played at birthday parties. Players take turns throwing the hammer at a large dragon drawn on a sheet of paper. They decide beforehand exactly where the beast must be hit, such as the heart or between the eyes. The player to come closest to the mark gets the first piece of birthday cake.

This is an especialy good game for older children to organize for younger ones.

For more information about target games and a list of other target games in this book, see page 38.

Pakistan
*Mazdoori

Playing area: A large, clear space, indoors or outdoors

Number of players: Four to thirty

Materials: None

Players are divided into two equal teams of two to 15 players each. For the first round of the game, the players on one team are the workers, those on the other the employers. Workers decide in secret what their trade or profession is. (They all choose the same one.) The workers then come toward the other team chanting, "If there is some work, let us do it. You will never find workers as good as us!"

They begin to pantomime their work, and the other team has to guess what it is. They have two guesses, and if they guess correctly, they become the workers for the next round of the game. If not, they remain the guessers.

For more information about drama and pantomime games and a list of other miming games in this book, see page 18.

Panama
El Peregrino
(The Pilgrim)

Playing area: Sidewalk, pavement, or hard, flat ground
Number of players: Two or more
Materials: Chalk to mark sidewalk or pavement; a flat marker for each player

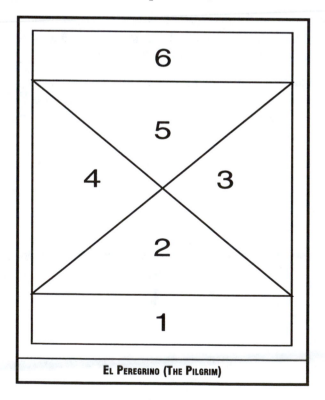

EL PEREGRINO (THE PILGRIM)

Players begin by marking the diagram on the playing surface. To decide who will go first, the players stand inside the first square and toss their markers toward square number six. The first player whose marker lands in that square begins the game.

A player kicks her marker into square one with her hopping foot, then hops into square one, then kicks the marker into square two, then hops into square two, and so on. After hopping into square four, she calls "rest," and puts her other foot down in square three. When she is ready, she continues kicking and hopping to square six, then back to the beginning, resting on four again if she wishes. Only players who complete a round successfully, without touching a line with the stone or the foot, continue into the next round. Play continues until only one player remains.

For more information about hopscotch and a list of other hopscotch games in this book, see page 25.

Papua New Guinea
Mailong Sera

Playing area: A space, outdoors or indoors, that is large enough for a circle of players
Number of players: Twelve to twenty
Materials: A smooth seashell, such as a cowry, around one inch in diameter

One player is chosen to be It. The other players stand or sit in a circle around It, very close to one another. It closes her eyes, and one of the players takes a shell in one of her hands. All of the players close their hands into loose fists, fingers down, and move their fists together until they touch, then apart so that they touch their neighbors' fists. It opens her eyes and the players in the circle move their hands back and forth to the rhythm of a song, trying to pass the seashell from hand to hand without It seeing who has the shell. Players who do not have the shell pretend to be fumbling with it. When It thinks she knows who has the shell, she calls the name of that player. If she is right, that player must take her place. If not, the passing begins again.

To keep the game interesting, you may want to limit It to three guesses before someone else takes his place at the center of the circle.

For more information about hide-and-seek and a list of other passing an object games in this book, see page 24.

Tomong Gilang Bogl Tondip
(Singing Tops)

Playing area: A hard dirt area, flat enough for top spinning, but soft enough so that small, pointed sticks can be pushed into the ground and made to stand up

Number of players: Two

Materials: Tops for each players (in New Guinea, tops for this game are made from sticks and nuts—children can make similar tops from a pencil and a ball of clay about the size of a walnut); ten short, thin sticks for each player

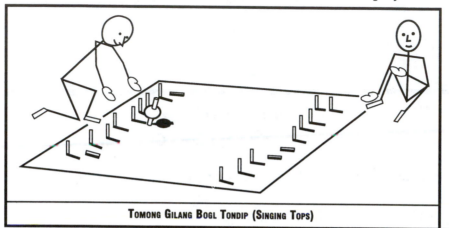

TOMONG GILANG BOGL TONDIP (SINGING TOPS)

This game was collected from the Chimbu people of central New Guinea. The players make their tops by burning a hole vertically through an acornlike nut and poking a sharpened stick through the hole. The pointed end of the stick extends only a short way through the bottom of the acorn.

Players mark a playing area, about six feet across and four feet wide, on the ground, then draw a line across the middle. Each player sets 10 thin sticks upright on his side of the playing area. The players take turns twirling a top between their palms and shooting it toward the opposite player's field. Whenever one player's stick is hit by a top, he lays that stick flat on the ground. The game continues until all of one player's sticks are lying on the ground.

A similar game is played by members of the Warao tribe of Guyana in South America, using a seed with a hard shell. Sometimes the seed is hollowed out and a hole drilled in the side, which makes the top hum as it spins. Because the New Guinea game is called "singing tops," it seems likely that their tops are hollowed out in this way also. To start the top spinning, the Warao pull on a string that has been wound around the stick and looped over the player's thumb. In their game, two or three players spin their tops at the same time on a wooden tray, and each tries to knock another's top off.

For more information about tops, see page 38.

120

Paraguay
*El Pan Quemado
(Burned Bread)

Playing area: A room with many good hiding places for objects

Number of players: At least two, but five or more is better

Materials: A blindfold

Everyone decides on an object to hide. It should be fairly large, about the size of a shoe. One player is blindfolded and leaves the room, while the others hide the object in plain sight. When the blindfolded player comes back, the others tell him, *"Se quema el pan"* (The bread is burning). He walks around the room, looking for the bread, and the others let him know how close he is by saying *"frío"* (cold), *"tibio"* (warm), *"caliente"* (hot), and, when he finds the bread, *"se quémo!"* (it's burned!).

For more information about hide-and-seek games and a list of other hidden object games in this book, see page 23.

Peru
*¿Lobo, Ya Estás?
(Wolf, Are You Ready?)

Playing area: A medium-sized, outdoor space with marked boundaries

Number of players: Ten or more

Materials: None

One player is chosen to play the part of the wolf, and she chooses a hiding place to be her den. The other players hold hands and form a circle around the den, then say, "Are you ready, Wolf, are you ready?"

The wolf answers, "I am just waking up."

Then the others repeat, "Are you ready, Wolf, are you ready?"

From this point, the wolf improvises until she is ready, saying things like "I'm putting on my shirt," or "I'm combing my hair." Whenever she chooses, she can answer, "Now I'm ready!" This is the signal that she will come out and chase the others, and the one she catches will then become the wolf in the next game. No player may run outside the game boundaries.

The place chosen for the wolf's den should be a hiding place under or behind something, so that the other players have a head start running away from her as she takes a moment to get out of her den. The wolf cannot begin to chase them until she has finished saying "Now I'm ready!"

A game like Wolf, Are You Ready? is played in England and other countries. In English, it is called What Time Is It, Mr. Wolf? The players keep asking the wolf what time it is, and he keeps answering with different times, such as 8:00, 8:15, and so on. Finally he calls out "It's dinner time!" and the chase begins.

For more information about tag and chasing games and a list of other Are You Ready? games in this book, see page 35.

El Reloj
(The Clock)

Playing area: A medium-sized, clear area, indoors or outdoors

Number of players: Six or more

Materials: A jump rope, fifteen to twenty feet long

Two players turn the ends of the rope. The others line up. One by one, they jump in, run out, and rejoin the line of players waiting to jump. The first player jumps once, saying, *"Es la una"* (It's one o'clock).

The second player jumps twice, saying, *"Son las dos"* (It's two o'clock), and so on, each player jumping the number of times of their hour, through 12 o'clock, then back to one o'clock.

For more information about jump-rope games and a list of other jump-rope games in this book, see page 27.

_____

Philippines
Hep

Playing area: Indoors or outdoors

Number of players: Three or more

Materials: None

One player is chosen as the storyteller, and he makes up a story about birds. Every time the listeners hear the name of a bird, they must say *"hep."* The storyteller tries to trick the listeners. He may try to make the story so exciting that the listeners forget to say *"hep."* Or he may try to make them say *"hep"* at the wrong time by using a word that only *sounds* like the name of a bird. (For instance, in English the story-teller could say "They were robin the bank," or "I think owl leave now.") Players who make a mistake are out of the game.

There are many, many different types of birds in the Philippines. Try to think of other categories besides birds that could be used to make a similar, challenging game for your group to play. Good categories for upper grades are names of television shows or of professional sports teams.

For more information about storytelling and word games and a list of other storytelling and word games in this book, see page 33.

Tabis-tabis

Playing area: A large, clear, outdoor space
Number of players: Five or more
Materials: A tin can; a different-colored wood block for each player

TABIS-TABIS

The players draw strings to decide who will be It. A player holds many strings of different lengths in cupped hands. The ends of the strings that the players can see seem to be the same length. The player who pulls the shortest string is It.

It places her wood block on the can, then draws a throwing line about 20 feet away from the can. The other players try, with their blocks, to knock It's block off the can. When one succeeds, he and all the unsuccessful players whose blocks lie on the ground run to pick them up, trying to return to the throwing line before It can put her block back on the can and tag them. If It tags a player, that player becomes It. If It does not tag a player, she is It for another round of the game.

For more information about tag and chasing games and a list of other tag and chasing games in this book, see page 37.

For more information about tag and chasing games and a list of other tag and chasing games in this book, see page 37.

Poland
Cymbergaj

Playing area: A tabletop, wide bench, or other smooth and level surface

Number of players: Two

Materials: Chalk; two coins, one large and one small; a small comb or a piece of stiff cardboard about the size of a small comb

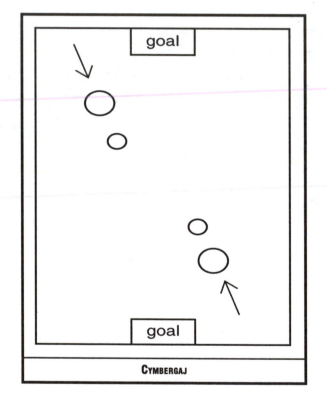

CYMBERGAJ

Players each take one of the short ends of the table or playing area, and each marks a rectangular goal box at the middle of his end. The object of the game is to push the large coin against the smaller one, moving the smaller one into the goal box (but not off the end of the table). Players turn their coins so that one player's coins are heads up, the other's tails up, so that they can tell them apart. The first player puts both coins near his own goal and pushes the large one toward the smaller one, using the comb or cardboard. Players alternate turns until one player reaches an agreed-upon number of goals.

124

Portugal
Jogo da Pedra
(Stone Game)

Playing area: A large, clear space outdoors

Number of players: Two or more

Materials: Nine large, flat stones; nine small, round stones; and nine more small, round stones for each player

Players lay the flat stones in a row and place a round stone on each one. They draw a line about 10 or 15 feet back and parallel to the row of stones. Players take turns throwing all nine of their stones at the small stones, scoring one point for each small stone that is knocked off its flat stone. Stones are reset before each new player's turn.

Games like this are played in many countries. The game is called Duck on a Rock in the United States.

For more information about target games and a list of other target games in this book, see page 38.

Romania
Ringlet Turns

Playing area: Indoors or outdoors

Number of players: Six or more

Materials: A ring

One player is chosen to be the game leader and another the guesser. The guesser bends forward, and each of the other players puts one finger on her back. The leader then puts the ring on a finger of one of the players and says, "Ringlet turns, guess whose finger I put it on."

If the guesser is correct, the player with the ring must take her place. If the guesser guesses incorrectly, she is thumped on the back by all the other players.

For more information about guessing games and a list of other Who Has It? games in this book, see page 21.

Russia
Czar and Peasants

Playing area: A large, clear space, indoors or outdoors
Number of players: Six or more
Materials: None

Draw two long parallel lines. Make them around 20 feet apart for younger children, farther apart for older children. One player is chosen to be the czar (or the czarina) and leaves the area while the peasants decide on a gift they will offer the royal person. The gift should be something they can easily and clearly mime as a group. It can be one large gift or many small gifts that are all the same. The czar returns and stands on one line while the peasants stand in a semicircle about five to 10 feet away. The peasants begin to mime what their gift is, showing how large it is, how it is used, etc. As soon as the czar guesses correctly, the peasants must all run and cross the far line before the czar tags them. If he fails to tag any of them, he is czar again, but if he tags any player, that player becomes czar or czarina.

For more information about drama and pantomime games and a list of other drama and pantomime games in this book, see page 18.

*Egg Rolling

Playing area: A clear space on the floor or smooth ground and next to a wall
Number of players: Two or more
Materials: Several hard-boiled eggs per player

Children play this game during Easter week. Players should be able to easily tell each others' eggs apart by markings or by color.

The players each place two or three eggs against a wall and draw a line a few feet back. Players will take turns rolling an egg from this line. The object of the game is to win the eggs of other players. To do so, a player's rolled egg must hit but not crack another player's egg. If the rolled egg cracks the egg that is hit, the owner of the cracked egg claims the egg that hit it. See page 48 for a game from Armenia using Easter eggs.

Ermine

Playing area: A small, clear space, indoors or outdoors
Number of players: Eight or more
Materials: An old leather belt

Players decide who will be It by grabbing onto the belt with one hand each, hand over hand. The last one who is able to grab the end of the belt becomes the ermine catcher. The belt, rolled and twisted into a tight ball, becomes the ermine.

An ermine is a small mammal that is prized and hunted for its fur. Russian children in long winter clothing would easily be able to hide the "ermine" under their legs in this game. Children in modern clothing will have to either play the game in semidarkness or drape blankets or coats over their knees.

The players sit in a tight circle with their knees drawn up, and the ermine catcher sits in the center. The ermine catcher closes her eyes and counts to 10 to give the players a chance to hide the ermine under one player's knees. When she opens her eyes, they begin frantically to pass (and pretend to pass) the ermine from one player to another. The ermine catcher turns from side to side, watches, listens, and tries to guess who has the ermine. When she does guess correctly, the person holding the ermine takes her place. In the Russia, players add excitement by trying to thump the ermine catcher whenever she has her back to the player who is holding it.

For more information about hide-and-seek and a list of other passing an object games in this book, see page 24.

Rwanda

Matha Kisana
(Jackstones)

Playing area: A small, clear space on soft ground or sand

Number of players: Two or more

Materials: Ten to twelve small fruit pits, such as cherry pits; a hard fruit or nut, about the size of a walnut, for each player to use as a taw

Matha Kisana is a jacks game played by children among the Thonga people. Players scoop out a hole in the ground the size of a shallow bowl and put the pits into it. In turn, each player sits close to the bowl and tosses the taw into the air. Very quickly and with only one hand, she scoops all the pits out of the bowl, shoves all but one back in, then catches the taw. She keeps doing this until all of the pits are out of the bowl. If she fails to get all the pits out of the bowl or leaves more or less than one out when she pushes the others back in, she loses her turn to the next player. If at any time her taw falls on the ground before she can catch it, she must toss a pit up in the air and catch it on the back of her hand, then toss it up from there and catch it in her palm to stay in the game at all (she still loses her turn).

On each new turn, a player begins with all the small pits in the hole, and the first player to complete the sequence of actions and get all the pits out of the hole is the winner

For more information about jacks games and a list of other jacks games in this book, see page 26.

Saudi Arabia
Marbles

Playing area: A smooth, clear dirt area

Number of players: Four or more

Materials: One marble per player

Players draw a throwing line, then dig a small hole about 15 to 20 feet away. The hole should be about four inches across and not too deep. They dig another hole five feet beyond the first, and another five feet beyond the second.

Each player needs one marble for this game, and they should all be different colors. To decide who goes first, players stand next to the first hole and throw or roll a marble toward the throwing line. The one whose marble lands closest to the line goes first, the second-closest goes second, and so on.

Players take one shot at a time and try to get their marble into the first hole, then the second, then the third. Then they reverse, shooting for the second hole, then the first hole, and continue in this way, back and forth. The first player to get his marble into the correct hole 10 times wins. Whenever a player gets a marble into a hole or hits another marble, he gets an extra turn. A player may choose to try to knock another player's marble far away rather than continue on course, especially if that player is ahead of him in the game.

For more information about marbles and a list of other marbles games in this book, see page 29.

Senegal
Lagan Buri

Playing area: A medium-sized, clear space, indoors or outdoors

Number of players: Six or more

Materials: A handkerchief, scarf, or small square of cloth

Players designate a home base and choose one player to hide the handkerchief (*lagan*), while the others cover their eyes. When the handkerchief has been hidden, the player who has hidden it gets away from the hiding place and calls, *"Buri."* The players then search for the handkerchief, and the one who finds it tries to tag as many players as possible before they can reach the home base. Tagged players are out of the game until the next round. It continues to hide the *lagan* until all players have been tagged.

For more information about hide-and-seek games and a list of other hidden object games in this book, see page 23.

---

*Mother, Mother, Tell Me the Time

Playing area: A clear space, at least ten by forty feet

Number of players: Four or more

Materials: None

One player is chosen to be the mother, and the others line up about 40 feet away. The players each take turns asking, "Mother, Mother, tell me the time." Mother answers with a number from one to 12, and that player may take that many steps toward the mother. The game ends when one of the players can touch the mother. That player becomes the mother, and the game begins again.

A similar game, Mother May I, is played in the United States. In Mother May I, the mother assigns different types of steps such as baby steps or giant steps.

*Shapza, Lapza, Who Is My Friend?

Playing area: A clear space, at least ten by twenty-five feet

Number of players: Four or more

Materials: None

One player is chosen to be It. He stands at one end of the playing area with his back turned to the other players, who stand side by side at the other end of the playing area. It holds his arms straight up above his head and says, "*Shapza, lapza*, who is my friend?" He claps his hands as he says this. While he is clapping, the other players walk toward him as quickly as they can. When he finishes the sentence, the players freeze. He turns quickly around and tries to catch one of the players moving. If It sees a player move, that player must return to the starting line. The first player to touch It while he is still saying *"Shapza, Lapza, who is my friend?"* takes his place, and the game begins again.

A game like this is one, known as Red Light, or Freeze, is played in the United States. In Russia, the game is known as Cats and Mice, and in Spain it is called Statues.

Slovak Republic
Trades

Playing area: Indoors or outdoors

Number of players: Six or more

Materials: None

This game is like North American Simon Says, but more complicated. One player is chosen as game leader, and she must pantomime an occupation while she tells who she is and what she is doing. For example, she says, "A baker kneads bread," or "A tailor sews," while pantomiming that kind of work. The other players must immediately copy her, and those who do not must pay a forfeit. (See Forfeits, page 19.) To fool the other players, the leader may say one occupation while miming another. Players may choose to either make no action or to mime the correct occupation. Any player who copies the leader's misleading actions must pay a forfeit.

For more information about drama and pantomime games and a list of other miming games in this book, see page 18.

South Africa
Diketo

Playing area: Outdoors, in sand or dirt

Number of players: Three to ten

Materials: Small stones, one for each player, and eight to ten to place in the central hole

This game was recorded among the Sotho people. Players dig the *sekhudu,* a hole about six inches across and two inches deep, in the ground or sand. The eight stones are put in the *sekhudu.* Before the game begins, players decide how many rounds will be played (usually two to 10) and which hand will be used, left or right. The first player to complete the agreed-upon number of rounds will be the winner. She makes a mark in the sand for each round she completes. An expert player can complete many rounds on just one turn. When a player makes a mistake, she loses her turn, and that round will not count for her.

The first player begins playing as the others watch. She takes one stone, the *moketo,* and tosses it up into the air. While it is in the air, she must take two or more of the eight stones, drag them out of the *sekhudu,* then catch the *moketo.*

130

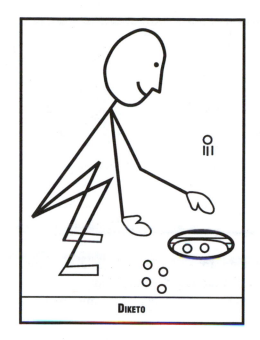

DIKETO

Then she throws the *moketo* up again, and pushes all but one of the stones back into the *sekhudu*, then catches the *moketo*. She continues in this way until only one stone remains in the *sekhudu*. She takes this one out and moves it around the *sekhudu* in six-inch jumps, throwing the *moketo* up before each move. Finally, she throws the *moketo* up, lays her palm flat on the ground so that the *moketo* lands and stays on top of it. This marks the end of one round. At the end of the last round, not only the last stone, but all eight are moved around the *sekhudu* in a circular pattern.

When a player is doing well, the others sing to her, calling her selfish, trying to make her lose her concentration.

For more information about jacks games and a list of other jacks games in this book, see page 26.

Dithwai

Playing area: Outdoors on soft dirt or sand

Number of players: Two to five

Materials: Each player needs ten to fifteen stones, about the size of a pigeon egg, each of a different color, shape, and markings

This game was recorded among the Sotho people. Each player builds a *lesaka,* a cattle pen, which is a flattened mound of dirt or sand about an inch high and six inches across. Players agree on how many cattle (stones) will be put in each pen.

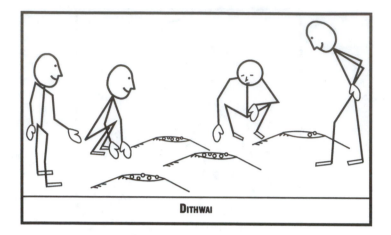

DITHWAI

Players choose their stones for their unique colors and markings. They take a few minutes to study their stones, then the first player closes his eyes as each of the others takes one of his stones and places it among their own. They say *"re a di thopa"* (we capture them) when they are finished, and the player opens his eyes and has to identify his cattle in each of the other pens. If he succeeds, he may take them back, but if he does not, he loses them. If he fails to find a single one, he must be It again. If he does find one or more, the first player in whose pen he recognized one of his cows becomes It. The game continues until the players are tired of playing, and the one with the most cattle at that time is the winner.

The skills needed to play *Dithwai* are the same skills that boys and young men use in their traditional jobs of guarding their families' cattle.

For more information about memory games and a list of other memory games in this book, see page 30.

Spain
Alquerque

Playing area: Anywhere

Number of players: Two

Materials: A piece of paper or other flat surface on which to draw a game diagram; twelve markers for each player

To begin the game, arrange the playing pieces on the game board as shown in the diagram.

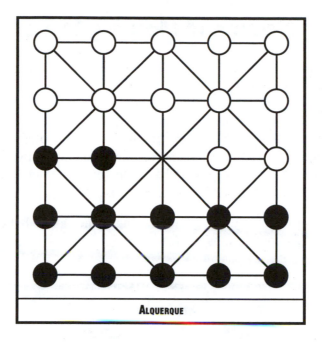

ALQUERQUE

Moves are made from one point (where lines cross) to an adjacent point. Pieces can be moved forward or to the side, but never backward. A player can capture an opponent's piece by jumping over it and landing on an empty point beyond. She can make a series of jumps, and she is allowed to change direction during jumps.

If a player misses an opportunity to jump an opponent's piece, her opponent removes the piece that should have made the jump from the board.

Once a player's marker reaches the opposite side of the board (the farthest row of points), it cannot move farther unless it can jump an opponent's marker (backwards). After such a jump, it is free to move forward or sideways as before.

A player wins when she has captured all of her opponent's markers or has blocked them so that they cannot move.

The earliest record of an *Alquerque* game is a diagram on a roofing tile of an Ancient Egyptian temple built around 1400 B.C. The game is called *El-quirkat* in Arabic and was mentioned in the 10th-century Moorish book, *Kitab al-Aghami*. *Alquerque* was described in the *Libro de Juegos* of King Alfonso the Learned of Castile, Spain, who had this beautifully illustrated book created in 1283. The Spanish introduced *Alquerque* into the Americas where it became very popular, especially in what is now the southwestern United States and Mexico. Two Native American *Alquerque* games are included in this book, the Zuni *Kolowis Awithlaknannai* and the Tarascan *El Coyote*.

For more information about board games and a list of other board games in this book, see page 14.

*Moon and Morning Stars

Playing area: A place where a tree casts long and interesting shadows

Number of players: Four to twenty

Materials: None

One player is chosen to be It (called the "moon"), while the others are the morning stars. The morning stars can run anywhere, but the moon must always have a foot on the tree's shadow. The stars run close and tease the moon. When the moon tags one of the morning stars, that player becomes the moon.

For more information about tag and chasing games and a list of other tag and chasing games in this book, see page 37.

Sri Lanka
Cheetah and Goats

Playing area: A large, outdoor space

Number of players: Seven to fifteen

Materials: None

One player is the cheetah, and the others form a line of goats, each holding onto the shoulders of the one in front. The cheetah says to the first goat, "I have come to eat a goat," and then he tries to tag the last goat in line.

The goats sing back, "Go and eat tasty goat droppings."

The first goat tagged must hold onto the shoulders of the cheetah, and the second holds onto the shoulders of the first, and so on. The game continues until all the goats have been captured.

The cheetah and the head goat should be two of the oldest and fastest players. This game works best with a mixed-age group.

For more information about tag and chasing games and a list of other line tag games in this book, see page 35.

Cows and Leopards

Playing area: Anywhere

Number of players: Two

Materials: A piece of paper or other flat surface on which to draw the game diagram; two markers for one player, and twenty-four for the other

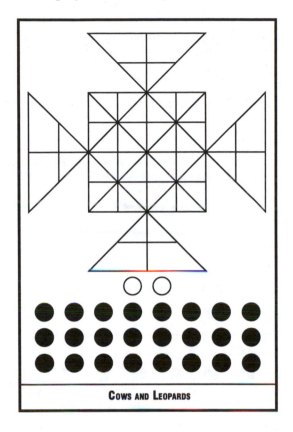

COWS AND LEOPARDS

This is a board game played by two players, each of whom has a different number of pieces and a different goal. One player has two leopards, the other has 24 cows. The leopards try to "eat" the cows by jumping over them and removing them from the board, and the cows try to crowd the leopards into a corner so that they cannot move.

The board is empty as the game begins. Players take turns placing and moving their markers. The markers are placed on the points where lines cross and may move one space along a line in any direction to the next point.

The player with the leopards begins by putting one leopard on the center point. The second player then puts one cow anywhere on the board. The first player places the second leopard anywhere on the board. Then the second player continues placing cows until all of them are on the board, alternating turns with the first player, who now moves either leopard one space at a time on each turn. No cow may be moved until all 24 are on the board, but the leopard may "eat" a cow by jumping over it at any time, as long as it can land on an empty point after the jump. The leopard may also make a series of jumps, as in checkers.

The cows win the game if they can force both leopards into a corner so that they cannot move; the leopards win if they can devour enough cows to keep from being trapped.

Once the leopards have eaten 10 cattle, it is unlikely they will ever be trapped, yet if the players are both experts, the cows will almost always win.

This game is also played in Nepal, where it is called *baagh-chaal* (tiger and goats).

For more information about board games and a list of other board games in this book, see page 14.

Sudan
Dala

Playing area: Anywhere

Number of players: Two

Materials: A piece of paper or other flat surface on which to draw the game diagram; twelve counters for each player

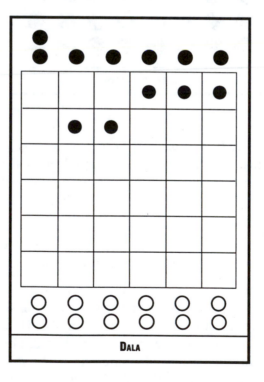

This game is played by the Bagara people. The game is often played on a diagram scratched in the dirt or mud, with a depression in the center of each square. When playing in mud, sticks are used as markers and stuck upright in the squares. Players

take turns placing their markers on the game board one at a time. The four center holes must be filled first. Then players may choose any empty square they wish. Any move that gives a player three markers in a row gives him the right to remove any one of the opposing player's markers from the board.

The black markers on the board in the diagram represent a "bull," which all players try to achieve. When a player has a bull, he can keep moving one stick back and forth, scoring three in a row each time, and there is nothing his opponent can do to stop him. A player who makes a bull on the board will tease his opponent by saying, "*tsp, tsp, tsp*," which is the noise a herdboy makes when leading a bull.

A player wins when he has taken all but two of his opponent's sticks.

A similar game called *Dara* is played in Nigeria.

For more information about board games and a list of other board games in this book, see page 14.

*Leopard Trap

Playing area: A large space, outdoors or indoors

Number of players: Thirty or more

Materials: None

Two players join their upraised hands, as in London Bridge, to form a leopard trap. The other players form a circle and run through the trap, singing and clapping. The words to the song are (in English translation):

Lion and leopard,
Lion and leopard,
Two night hunters.
Lion and leopard,
Lion and leopard,
Trap their prey!

On the last word of the song, the trap falls and the two players catch the player running through, who drops out of the game. When a second player is trapped, the two trapped players form a second bridge-trap along the circle. This continues until only two players remain in the game.

For more information about London Bridge games and a list of other London Bridge games in this book, see page 28.

Sweden
Numbers Tag

Playing area: A large, paved area

Number of players: Eight or more

Materials: Chalk to mark pavement

Players decide on the boundaries of the playing area and choose one player to be It. The other players huddle far from It while It turns around and covers his ears. The players count off, so that each one has a number that she or he will use throughout the game. Then the players scatter, and each chooses a place to stand and draws a circle on the ground. The circle should be about four feet across.

When the players are in place, It stands at the edge of the playing area, at any spot he wishes, and calls out two numbers. The players with those numbers must run quickly to each other's circles. It tries to get into one of the empty circles first. If he fails, he calls out two more numbers. He may not call either of the two numbers he has just called. When he does manage to get into an empty circle, the player without a circle becomes It.

Players will need to choose new numbers at the end of every game, or every few games.

For more information about tag and chasing games and a list of other exchanging places games in this book, see page 36.

Switzerland
Hallihallo

Playing area: A fairly large space, outdoors or indoors.

Number of players: Six to twenty

Materials: A medium-sized rubber ball (a beanbag or similar soft object could be used indoors)

One player is chosen to be game leader, and the others line up one behind the other, facing the leader at a distance of eight feet or more. The leader decides on the name of an animal, then says (for example), "Name the animal, first letter A" (or whatever the first letter is of the animal he has chosen). Quickly, she throws the ball to the player at the front of the line, who must say the name of an animal that begins with "A" without hesitating. If the guess is correct, that player becomes It. If the guess is wrong, or the player cannot think of a name, that player goes to the end of the line, and the leader repeats, "Name the animal, first letter A." If everyone in the line fails to guess, the leader starts again at the beginning of the line, this time giving the first two letters of the animal's name.

For more information about category games and a list of other category games in this book, see page 15.

─────────────────────────────

Syria
*Don't Laugh

Playing area: A clear space, indoors or outdoors, where players can sit in a circle on the floor, on the ground, or in chairs

Number of players: Eight or more

Materials: None

Players sit in a circle, and choose one player to be the leader. The leader makes a movement, and each of the players in turn around the circle must copy it. Anyone who laughs or makes a noise is out of the game. The last player left, who has neither laughed nor spoken, becomes the leader for the next game.

For other laughing games, see United States: The Prince of Morocco, and United States (Native American—Nootka): Laughing Games.

─────────────────────────────

Tanzania
Giant's House

Playing area: A medium-sized, clear space

Number of players: Thirteen or more

Materials: None

One player is chosen to be the game leader, and the rest are divided into groups of four or five. Each group chooses a corner or part of the room, which they will use later in the game.

All join hands and circle around the leader chanting, "Come inside the giant's house, and say what you can see."

Then the leader names an object in the giant's house, for example, "I can see a snake."

Players hurry to their designated parts of the room, and each group works together to form that object with their bodies. The leader chooses the one he likes best, and a player from that group becomes the new leader.

For more information about drama and pantomime games and a list of other drama and pantomime games in this book, see page 18.

Thailand
Takraw

Playing area: A clear space, indoors or outdoors, large enough for the circle of players

Number of players: Four or more

Materials: A very light ball, four to six inches in diameter (try a hollow plastic ball or, for young children, a thick balloon)

The traditional *takraw* ball is woven of rattan. It is two to four inches in diameter and hollow. They are available at some import shops. *Takraw* is played by teams of adults on a court and is a very popular spectator sport in parts of southeast Asia. A similar game called *Chinlon* is played in Myanmar (Burma), and another called *Sepak Raga Bulatan* is played in Malaysia.

Children play a much simpler version of the game. They stand in a circle and try to keep the ball in the air as long as possible, hitting it with any part of their bodies except the arms. Sometimes the players keep score. Players take penalty points each time they let the ball fall to the ground, and the player with the lowest score when playing stops is the winner. The game may also be played by one person, who tries to keep the ball in the air while counting the number of successful hits.

For more information about shuttlecock games and a list of other shuttlecock games in this book, see page 32.

Tibet
Wolf and Sheep

Playing area: A large, open, outdoor space or gymnasium

Number of players: Seven or more

Materials: None

This game comes from the Kham people of western Tibet. Children form a line, each holding onto the clothing of the player in front. These are the sheep, and the first one in line is the mother sheep. Another player has been chosen as the wolf, and the wolf tries to catch the last player in line. The mother sheep tries to keep her lambs away from him. Whenever the wolf catches the last player in line, that lamb has been "eaten" and must leave the game.

This game works best with a mixed-age group.

For more information about tag and chasing games and a list of other line tag games in this book, see page 35.

Togo

*Awako

(The Hawk)

Playing area: A large, rectangular playing area.

Number of players: Eight or more

Materials: Chalk to mark lines on playing area, if it is paved, or something to draw lines in the dirt or sand

Draw lines to mark the playing area into three sections lengthwise. The center area should be much larger than the end areas. Two players are selected as hawk and hen. The remaining players play the part of the hen's chicks. The hen stands in one end section of the field and the chicks stand in the other, with the hawk in the middle. The hen calls out, "Little chicks, come here!" The chicks run toward the hen. The hawk pursues them with wings outstretched and tries to tag as many as possible. The chicks who are tagged are out of the game. Then the hen moves to the other side of the field, and the game begins again. This continues until all the chicks have been caught. If there are a lot of players, the game will go faster (and the hawk will not become exhausted) if the tagged chicks are transformed into hawks and help catch the other chicks.

For more information about tag and chasing games and a list of other tag and chasing games in this book, see page 37.

Trinidad and Tobago

Trier

Playing area: A clear area, indoors or outdoors, on the floor or ground

Number of players: Two or more

Materials: Five jackstones (small flat pebbles)

In the first round of play, each player, in turn, tosses all five stones up in the air and catches as many as he can on the back of his hand. A player's score is the number of jackstones successfully caught in this way. Three rounds are played, and the player with the highest score has the first turn in the next round, the one with the second highest score has the second turn, and so on.

In the second round, a player tosses the five stones up in the air and catches as many as possible on the back of her hand. Then she tosses again, and must catch all of the tossed stones in her palm. If she misses any at all on this toss, her score is zero. If she does not miss, she lays four stones on the ground, and tosses the fifth one in the air, and picks up one with the same hand, catching the tossed stone before it hits the ground. She continues until she has picked up all four stones. The first player to complete this round without a mistake is the winner. A player who makes a mistake loses her turn and must start again at the beginning of round two on her next turn.

For more information about jacks games and a list of other jacks games in this book, see page 26.

Turkey
Fox and Hen

Playing area: A large, open outdoor space
Number of players: Seven to fifteen
Materials: None

One player is chosen to play the part of the fox, and he marks off a square at the edge of the playing area as his den. Another player is the hen. The other players—the chicks—line up behind the hen, each holding onto the shoulders or waist of the player in front. The fox walks up to the hen and asks for the last chick in line by name. The hen refuses, and tries to keep in front of the fox and keep him from grabbing or tagging the last chick.

When the fox has caught the last chick (and the game would not be any fun unless he did), he leads the chick to his den, then returns and asks the hen for the next chick. The hen can release her stolen chick by going over to the den and touching him. The chicks must stay inside the den, but they may stretch out their hands to make it easier for the hen to touch them. Once tagged, the chicks run quickly to rejoin the line. The game ends when the fox has taken all the chicks, or when the hen has lost all but one chick and then won all of them back.

This game works best with a mixed-age group. The roles of the fox and the hen should be taken by two of the older, more skillful players.

For more information about tag and chasing games and a list of other line tag games in this book, see page 35.

How Do You Like Your Neighbor?

Playing area: A medium-sized, clear area, indoors or outdoors

Number of players: Fifteen or more

Materials: None

One player is chosen to be It, and the other players sit in a circle around him. They may sit on chairs or on the floor. If they sit on the floor, they should be very close together so that when a player leaves her place, it is obvious where the empty space is. It stands in the center of the circle and asks another player, "How do you like your neighbor?" The player may answer either "Fine" or "Not at all." If the answer is "Not at all," the seated player calls out the name of another player, and the two quickly change places. The center player tries to get into one of the empty chairs or places first. If he succeeds, the player who no longer has a seat becomes It.

For more information about tag and chasing games and a list of other exchanging places games in this book, see page 36.

Uganda
Inzama

Playing area: A large, flat, outdoor space

Number of players: Three or more

Materials: A large ball; a fairly harmless stick, such as a hardwood dowel, for each thrower to use as a spear (paint or mark the spears with different colors, so that you can tell whose spear hit the ball)

Draw a line, 20 feet long or longer, which will be the line where players stand when throwing spears. Draw another line parallel to the first, 10 to 15 feet away. Two players stand at either end of the second line and roll the ball back and forth. The ball represents an antelope, and the players try to spear it with their sticks. Each player scores a point for each hit.

In Uganda, the game was traditionally played with a large pumpkin and real, sharp spears. Players' spears had to pierce the skin of the pumpkin.

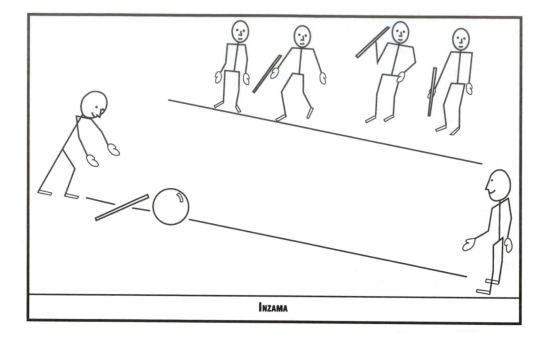

INZAMA

For more information about target games and a list of other target games in this book, see page 38.

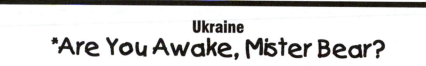

Ukraine
*Are You Awake, Mister Bear?

Playing area: A large, rectangular space outdoors

Number of players: Six or more

Materials: None

Players mark an area at one corner of the rectangle as Mister Bear's den and a larger area at the opposite corner as "home," a safe area for the children who are teasing Mister Bear.

This is a tag game. One player is chosen to be It, or "Mister Bear." The bear lies down in his den and pretends to sleep. The other players come close to the den and ask, "Are you awake, Mister Bear?" They ask the question again and again, first in soft voices, then louder and louder, but the bear snores and pretends not to hear them. Finally, when Mister Bear decides that the players are off their guard, he shouts "Yes!" and jumps up and tries to tag as many as he can before they reach their safe zone. The bear may only begin the chase after the players finish asking the question. Players who are tagged become bear cubs, join the bear in his den, and help him tag the others. The game continues until all the players have been captured.

For more information about tag and chasing games and a list of other Are You Ready? games in this book, see page 35.

Hopscotch

Playing area: Sidewalk, pavement, or hard, flat ground

Number of players: Two or more

Materials: Chalk to mark sidewalk or pavement; a flat marker for each player

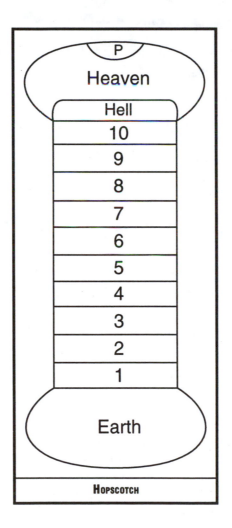

HOPSCOTCH

The first player stands on Earth and tosses her marker into block one. She then hops into block one, picks up the marker, tosses it to Earth, and hops back to Earth. In the second round, she tosses the marker into block number two, hops into block number one, then into block number two, picks up her marker, tosses it to Earth, and so on until she reaches block 10. The player then tosses the marker into Heaven, hops there (skipping over Hell), then begins the game again from Heaven, completing the entire game from there back to Earth.

If a player's foot or marker touches a line, if the marker lands in the wrong place, or if her lifted foot touches the ground, she loses her turn and begins her next turn on the round she missed. If the marker or a player's foot lands in Hell, not only does the player lose a turn, but she must start over from the very beginning on her next turn. If her marker lands in the Post (P) section of Heaven, she is not allowed to speak or laugh for the rest of the game; if she does, she is out of the game.

After successfully completing this circuit, the player hops the whole pattern once in each of the following ways:

1. while balancing the marker on her upraised foot

2. while balancing the marker on her forefinger

3. while balancing the marker on top of her head

4. with her eyes closed

Players often make up other peculiar ways to hop.

For more information about hopscotch and a list of other hopscotch games in this book, see page 25.

Monday, Tuesday

Playing area: A good ball-bouncing wall

Number of players: Seven

Materials: A small- to medium-sized rubber ball that will bounce well against a wall

Each of the seven players counts off with the name of a day of the week. Sunday begins the game by throwing the ball against the wall. Just as the ball leaves Sunday's hands, she calls the name of another day of the week, and that person must catch the ball before it bounces. If he succeeds in catching the ball, he throws it against the wall and calls the name of another day. If a player misses the ball the thrower must pick up the ball then throw it at any other player. A player who has been tagged three times in this way is out of the game.

For more information about ball games and a list of other ball games in this book, see page 12. For more information about tag and chasing games and a list of other tag and chasing games in this book, see page 37.

Three Men's Morris

Playing area: Anywhere

Number of players: Two

Materials: A piece of paper or other flat surface on which to draw the game board; three markers for each player

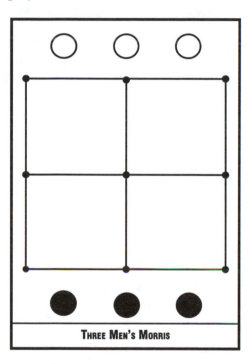

THREE MEN'S MORRIS

This game is similar to Tic Tac Toe. At the beginning of the game, the board is empty. Each player takes a turn placing one piece at a time on any vacant point. After all the pieces have been placed, the players take turns moving one of their markers to any empty point on the board until one player gets three pieces in a straight line, vertically, horizontally, or diagonally.

The earliest playing diagram for a Morris game can be seen on a roofing slab of an ancient Egyptian temple at Kurna, which was built around 1400 B.C. In about 500 B.C., the Chinese played the game and called it *Yih.* Morris games were very popular in medieval and Renaissance England. Designs for more difficult versions of the game—Six Men's and Nine Men's Morris—have been found carved in the pavement in ancient Greece, Rome, and Crete. In many countries where this game is found, its name sounds very much like the Latin word *merellus,* which means "coin" or "token." The game is known as *Merelles* in France; Merrymen, Merryholes, and Morris in England; *Muhle* in Germany; *Mlyn* in the Czech Republic and Slovakia; and *Melnitsa* in Russia.

For more information about board games and a list of other board games in this book, see page 14.

Scotland
Albert Adams Ate an Alligator

Playing area: Anywhere

Number of players: Two or more

Materials: None

Every player must make up a sentence of exactly five words, and each word must begin with the same letter of the alphabet. The first player begins with the letter "A," saying a sentence such as "Albert Adams ate an alligator." The next player continues by making up a sentence of five words beginning with the letter "B."

Players compete to see who can make up the most original sentences with the least hesitation. Any player who cannot give a sentence, or who uses an incorrect letter, must pay a forfeit. (See Forfeits, page 19.) Players may want to decide in advance not to use certain difficult letters such as "X" and "Z," or to allow players to add extra small words such as "a," "an," and "the."

For more information about storytelling and word games and a list of other storytelling and word games in this book, see page 33.

Wales
How Many Fingers?

Playing area: Indoors or outdoors

Number of players: Three or more

Materials: Blindfold

One player is blindfolded and stands with his face toward a wall. A second player jumps on his back and holds up a certain number of fingers, saying, "Buck shee, buck shee buck, how many fingers do I hold up?"

The first player must guess the number of fingers, and a third player makes sure that there is no cheating. If the first player guesses correctly, he and the second player change places; if not, he must guess again.

For more information about guessing games and a list of other How Many Fingers? games in this book, see page 21.

United States
A, My Name Is Alice

Playing area: A small, open space with hard floor or ground for ball bouncing

Number of players: One or more

Materials: A rubber ball, large or small, that the player can easily bounce with one hand

This game challenges a player to make up variations on a folk rhyme while bouncing a ball in rhythm to the words. In addition, he must bounce the ball under the leg on every word that begins with the key letter of the rhyme. Players go through the alphabet, reciting the following for each letter:

> A, my name is Alice,
> My (husband's/wife's/mother's/father's) name is (name beginning with A),
> I come from (a place beginning with the letter A),
> and we sell (something that begins with the letter A).

Players must remember to bounce the ball under their leg on every single word in the rhyme that begins with the key letter, even tiny words such as "a," "I," and "is." A player loses her turn when she misses, and on her next turn she begins on the letter she missed.

This game has been made into a picture book, *A, My Name Is Alice*, by Jane Bayer, illustrated by Steven Kellogg (Dial, 1984). The rhyme is also used in jumping rope.

For more information about storytelling and word games and a list of other storytelling and word games in this book, see page 33. For more information about ball games and a list of other ball games in this book, see page 12.

Categories

Playing area: A space where players can sit in a circle

Number of players: Four or more

Materials: None

Players sit in a circle and clap in unison to the following pattern:

> Clap both hands on thighs twice
> Clap hands together twice
> Snap fingers of left hand
> Snap fingers of right hand
> Repeat pattern

One player begins the game by naming a category on the "snap, snap" portion of the pattern. Popular categories are car names, rock bands, football teams, etc. Without missing a beat and without repeating items, each player in turn must name something from that category. A player who does not name something from that category on the "snap, snap" of the next clap is out, and so is a player who names something that does not fit the category or one who repeats an item already mentioned.

For more information about category games and a list of other category games in this book, see page 15.

Categories Hopscotch

Playing area: Sidewalk, pavement, or hard, flat ground
Number of players: Two or more
Materials: Chalk to mark sidewalk or pavement; a flat marker for each player

movie stars	monsters
colors	TV shows
cars	states
boys' names	girls' names

CATEGORIES HOPSCOTCH

Each player must hop the alphabet. On the first round, each player names an item in each category beginning with the letter "A," then "B," etc. Players usually decide which letters to skip and how long a player may stand in a square before naming something from that category. A player loses his turn if he steps on a line, puts his lifted foot down, or cannot think of an item for the category. Players make up their own categories, and the hopscotch diagrams can have any number of squares.

For more information about hopscotch and a list of other hopscotch games in this book, see page 25. For more information about category games and a list of other category games in this book, see pages 14–15.

Chick-ur-mur Cravy Crow

Playing area: A large space, indoors or outdoors

Number of players: Six or more

Materials: None

One of the players is the witch, one is hen, and the rest are chicks. The witch squats on the ground and pretends to be searching for something in the dirt. The others stand in a line, each holding onto the shoulders or waist of the player in front. All march around the Old Witch, chanting the following:

> Chick-ur-mur, chick-ur-mur, cravy crow,
> Went to the well to wash my toe,
> When I came back my chicken was gone
> What time is it, old witch?
> The witch answers, "One."

The children march around and repeat the chant 11 times in all, until the witch names the witching hour of 12. Then the player at the head of the line, the Old Hen, has a conversation with the witch:

Old Hen: What are you looking for, Old Witch?

Old Witch: Grandmother's darning needle.

Old Hen: When did she lose it?

Old Witch: Last deep snow.

Old Hen: Is this it?

The hen shows one foot, then the other, and the other players follow her actions, one after another, down the line. The witch says "no" to all the players except the last one, whom she chases. The chicks scatter, and the hen tries to defend them. The first chick caught takes a turn being the Old Witch.

Games very similar to this one have been played in England, Scotland, and throughout the United States. According to folklorist Zora Neale Hurston, this game was once especially popular among African American children.

For more information about tag and chasing games and a list of other line tag games in this book, see page 35.

Fizz-Buzz

Playing area: Any space where players can sit in a circle in chairs or on the ground

Number of players: At least four, but ten or more is best

Materials: None

One player begins counting with the number one, and the other players count off around the circle in a clockwise direction. Players must say the word "fizz" in place of the number five or any multiple of the number five, and the word "buzz" in place of the number seven or any multiple of the number seven. For instance, they would say, "One, two, three, four, *fizz*, six, *buzz*, eight, nine, *fizz*, eleven, twelve, thirteen, *buzz, fizz*," and so on. The numbers 35 and 70 will both be "fizz-buzz."

Some traditional variations intended to make the game harder are saying "quack" for 12 and multiples of 12, and saying "fizz" for 50 and "fizz-one" for 51, and "buzz" for 70, and "buzz-one" for 71, and so on.

For more information about number and counting games and a list of other number and counting games in this book, see page 30.

Fox and Geese

Playing area: A large, flat, open, snowy space

Number of players: Five or more

Materials: None

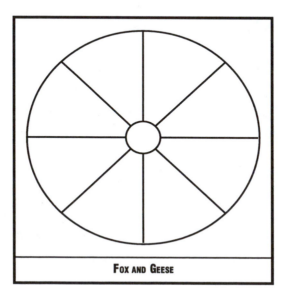

FOX AND GEESE

This is a tag game, and one player is chosen to be It (the fox). The other players are the geese. The players draw a large figure in the snow that looks like a wheel with a hub and spokes. All players must stay on the lines of the wheel. In some variations of the game, the geese can run on the circle or the spokes, but the fox can only run on the spokes. In others versions, the hub of the wheel is called the "chicken coop," and it is a safety area for the geese. However, if too many geese stay there for too long, the fox may insist on a time limit or a limit to the number of geese that can be there at one time. When the fox tags a goose, the goose becomes the new fox.

For more information about tag and chasing games and a list of other tag and chasing games in this book, see page 37.

*Head of the Class

Playing area: A stairway that is wide enough for all the players to sit side by side, and with not too many steps, unless you want the game to last a long time

Number of players: Three to five

Materials: A small pebble or similar object

One player is chosen to be the teacher. The other players sit or stand side by side on the lowest step. The teacher hides the pebble in one fist, then asks the first player to guess where it is. If the player guesses correctly, he may move up one step. The teacher continues to hide the pebble and asks the players in turn to guess which hand it is in. The first player to reach the top step wins the game.

For more information about guessing games and a list of other Who Has It? games in this book, see page 21.

Jacks

Playing area: A flat, clear space on floor, dirt, or pavement

Number of players: Two or more

Materials: Five store-bought jacks or small flat stones

These jacks games were popular over a hundred years ago and are played without a ball. Instead, one of the jacks is tossed up in the air and caught.

Horses in the Stable. A player places her left hand on the table with the fingers spread out. Each time she tosses one jack into the air, she pushes one on the ground into each of the four "V" openings made by the fingers.

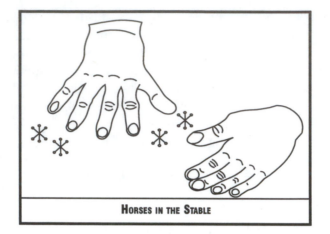

HORSES IN THE STABLE

Peas in the Pod. A player holds the left hand on the table, fingertips down, with the ends of the thumb and forefinger joined in a circle. He scatters four jacks. He tosses the fifth jack up, pushes one of the four jacks into the left hand, then catches the tossed jack. He continues until all four peas are in the pod. Then he moves the left hand, throws one jack up, picks up the other four, and catches the tossed jack.

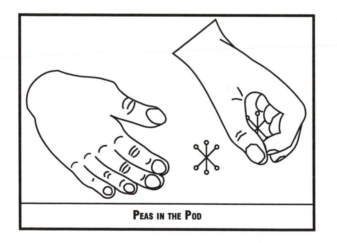

PEAS IN THE POD

Riding the Elephant. A player places four jacks in a line with about an inch between them. The player puts the fifth jack on the back of her hand and traces a curved line in and out among the four with her forefinger. Then she tosses up the jack on her hand, picks up all the others, and catches the tossed jack before it hits the ground, all with one hand.

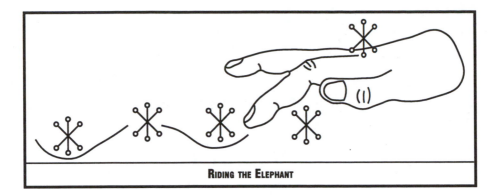

RIDING THE ELEPHANT

For more information about jacks games and a list of other jacks games in this book, see page 26.

Jump Rope

Playing area: Pavement, sidewalk, or hard dirt

Number of players: At least three

Materials: A rope, fifteen to twenty feet long

Two players each grasp an end of the rope with one hand and turn their hands in a circle high enough so that the middle of the rope rises above the height of the jumper. Following the rhythm of the rope, jumpers enter, do tricks, and exit while chanting rhymes to the rhythm of the rope.

The rhymes often ask a question that is answered with a number. For instance:

Cinderella, dressed in yella,
Went upstairs to kiss a fella.
By mistake she kissed a snake.
Came downstairs with a bellyache.
How many doctors did it take?

At the end of the question, the turners turn the rope as fast as they can (called "red hot peppers"), and everyone counts how many times the jumper can jump without missing.

Other jump-rope rhymes suggest the motions a jumper must make. In "Teddy Bear," players must perform all the teddy bear's motions as they jump, then jump out on "good night."

Teddy bear, teddy bear, turn around.
Teddy bear, teddy bear, touch the ground.
Teddy bear, teddy bear, tie your shoes.
Teddy bear, teddy bear, read the news.
Teddy bear, teddy bear, go upstairs.

Teddy bear, teddy bear, say your prayers.
Teddy bear, teddy bear, turn out the light.
Teddy bear, teddy bear, say goodnight.

More advanced jumpers will then jump very fast as they spell out G-O-O-D-N-I-G-H-T.

For more information about jump-rope games and a list of other jump-rope games in this book, see page 27.

Lemonade

Playing area: A large, open space, indoors or outdoors

Number of players: At least ten

Materials: None

Players mark two parallel lines, about 25 feet across and wide enough to allow all the players on a team to line up side by side. The players divide into two teams, and the teams go to opposite lines. One team pantomimes first. Together, they decide on an occupation they will act out for the other team to guess. When they are ready, they start the following exchange:

Mimers: Bum, bum, here we come!
Guessers: Where from?
Mimers: New York! [or wherever the players live]
Guessers: What's your trade?
Mimers: Lemonade!
Guessers: Show us how you do it if you're not afraid!

The miming team walks toward the guessing team's line while pretending to do some kind of work. The guessers stand behind their line, saying aloud what they think the other team's occupation is. As soon as they guess the type of work, the mimers turn and run back to their line, while the guessers try to tag them. All the players who are tagged must join the other team. It is now the guessing team's turn to mime and the miming team's turn to guess.

If a team gets all the way to their opponents' line before their trade is guessed, they return to their line (not having lost any players), and the other team begins miming a trade. The game is over when all or nearly all players are on one team.

For more information about drama and pantomime games and a list of other miming games in this book, see page 18.

Marbles

Playing area: A flat, dirt area

Number of players: Three or more

Materials: Ten or more marbles for each player

Here are three different versions of marbles.

Bridgeboard. Books of children's games often describe a game in which players roll their marbles at the holes in a bridgeboard and score the number of points above a hole if their marble goes inside. Supposedly, players kept score and the player with the highest score won. In the real world of the streets, bridgeboard games were made and set up by young entrepreneurs, who promised confident shooters to pay the number of marbles above each hole if the player's marble went inside. If the player missed, the owner kept the marble, and the odds were nearly always in the owner's favor.

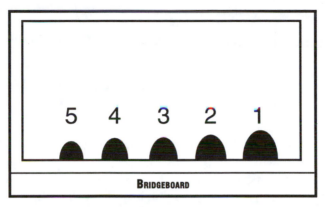

BRIDGEBOARD

Old Bowler. This traditional marble game was a favorite of Abraham Lincoln. Players draw a square about 12 to 14 inches on the sides, in the dirt. Then they draw two lines connecting the corners and a starting line a few feet back from one side of the square. They place their marbles at the four corners and in the center. Players roll their marbles from the starting line, a few feet back, and the player whose marble lands closest to near side of the square shoots first. Players try to hit the four corner marbles, then the center marble, the "old bowler." Each player shoots until she misses. If a player, by mistake, hits the old bowler before the other four marbles have been taken, that player is out of the game.

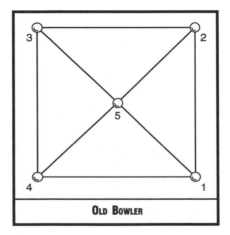

OLD BOWLER

Ring Game. Players draw a ring, about six feet across, on the ground with a finger, pointed stick, or stone. They draw a line six or seven feet away from the edge of the circle.

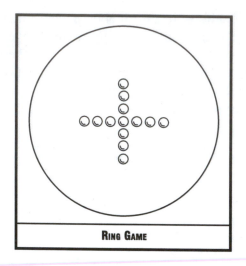

RING GAME

Each player puts the same number of marbles in the ring. The size of the ring, the number of marbles the players place in it, and the distance they place them from the starting line may vary. The diagram shows a regulation tournament setup, but players may arrange the marbles any way they choose.

All the players stand on the starting line and shoot a marble toward the ring; the one whose marble comes closest to the edge of the ring shoots first. The players take turns trying to knock one or more of the marbles out of the ring. A player keeps shooting as long as he hits a marble and as long as his shooter remains in the ring, beginning each time from the spot where his shooter rested after it was shot. When playing for keeps, a player takes any marbles he shoots out of the ring.

For more information about marbles and a list of other marbles games in this book, see page 29.

"May I?" Hopscotch

Playing area: Sidewalk, pavement, or hard, flat ground

Number of players: Two or more

Materials: Chalk to mark sidewalk or pavement

A players closes his eyes or looks upward as he hops from square to square in number order. After each hop, he asks, "May I?" If the player has landed in the correct space without touching a line, another player answers "yes," but if the

```
┌─────────────────────────┐
│  ┌───────────┬─────────┐ │
│  │     3     │    4    │ │
│  ├───────────┼─────────┤ │
│  │     2     │    5    │ │
│  ├───────────┼─────────┤ │
│  │     1     │    6    │ │
│  └───────────┴─────────┘ │
│     "MAY I?" HOPSCOTCH    │
└─────────────────────────┘
```

player has hopped outside the square or onto a line, the other player says "no." When a player has gone around successfully facing forward, he attempts another round jumping backwards.

For more information about hopscotch and a list of other hopscotch games in this book, see page 25.

Miss Mary Mack

Playing area: Anywhere
Number of players: Two or more
Materials: None

Hand clapping can be done to the rhythm of playground rhymes or to the lyrics of popular songs. In some games, two players face each other; in others, three or more players form a circle.

One of the most basic series of claps for two players is as follows:

Clap both hands together

Clap each other's right hand

Clap hands together

Clap each other's left hand

Clap hands together

Clap both of each other's hands

Clap hands together

Cross hands and touch chest

159

Clap both hands on knees

(Begin again)

This series can be done while chanting "Miss Mary Mack," an old American folk rhyme. One complete clapping series is done to each line of the poem.

Miss Mary Mack, Mack, Mack,
All dressed in black, black, black,
With silver buttons, buttons, buttons,
All down her back, back, back.
She cannot read, read, read,
She cannot write, write, write,
But she can smoke, smoke, smoke,
Her daddy's pipe, pipe, pipe.
She asked her mother, mother, mother,
For 50 cents, cents, cents,
To see the elephant, elephant, elephant,
Jump over the fence, fence, fence.
He jumped so high, high, high,
He touched the sky, sky, sky,
And he didn't come back, back, back,
Till the fourth of July, ly, ly.

The first four lines of "Miss Mary Mack" were originally a riddle, for which the answer was "a coffin."

For more information about hand-clapping games, see page 22.

*Peggy in the Ring

Playing area: A small, open space, indoors or outdoors

Number of players: Ten or more

Materials: A cane or staff; a blindfold

One player is chosen to be It and is blindfolded. The other players form a ring around him, holding hands and circling around. It holds a cane or staff in one hand. When he strikes the floor three times with the staff, all the others must stand still. It points the staff toward the circle, and the person closest to the tip must grab it. "Squeak!" It commands, and the player at the other end must make a squeaking sound. Then It guesses who has squeaked. If he is right, that player takes his place. If he is wrong, he is It for another game.

In another version from the United States, It commands the person to make the noise of a certain animal.

For more information about guessing games and a list of other Who Was It? games in this book, see page 20.

The Prince of Morocco

Playing area: A space, indoors or outdoors, where players can sit in a circle

Number of players: Five or more

Materials: None

One player is chosen to be It, and the others sit in a circle around her. The object of the game is for It to make one of the other players laugh without laughing herself, while the player tries to make It laugh. It approaches one of the players, and the two of them say the following:

> It: The Prince of Morocco is dead, is dead.
>
> Player: I'm sorry to hear it. I'm sorry to hear it.
>
> It: He died of the gout in his big left toe.
>
> Player: I'm sorry to hear it. I'm sorry to hear it.

Then they shake hands very hard while both saying, "Good evening, good evening, good evening."

If It laughs first, or if neither one laughs, she must remain It and begin again. If the player laughs first, he becomes It.

See the other laughing games in this book, Syria: Don't Laugh, and United States (Native American—Nootka): Laughing Games.

Skelly

Playing area: Sidewalk or pavement

Number of players: Three or more

Materials: Chalk; one playing piece for each person (bottle caps or plastic checkers work well, though bottle caps need to be filled with clay or melted candle wax to make them heavier)

Players draw the diagram on the sidewalk or pavement. It should be about six feet wide on each side, if there is enough space. A starting line is drawn about 15 feet back from the skelly diagram. Players shoot their markers by holding the forefinger under the thumb and flicking the forefinger at the marker.

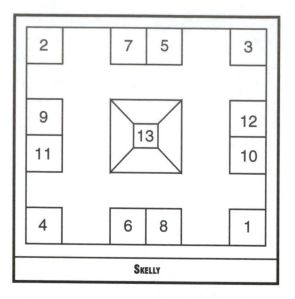

The first player shoots from the starting line to square 1 and keeps shooting as long as he gets from one number to the next in one shot without landing on a line. If he fails to do this, he loses his turn, but he does not lose his place on the skelly diagram. If a player chooses, he can shoot another player's marker as far as possible instead of taking a shot at the next number. In some games, a player needs to hit another player's marker to earn the right to flick it as far away as possible.

Players go from square 1 to square 13 and back to square 1 again. Once a player reaches square 1, he becomes a "killer," and must hit all the other markers before winning the game.

In his book, *What Did You Do When You Were a Kid?* Fred Sturmer recalls that he and his friends would decide who would shoot first in Skelly in the following way. One of them would say, "Who wants to play Skelly?" then the first kid to say "Larry" would go first, the second one to say "Larry" would shoot second, and so on.

Twelve Days of Christmas

Playing area: Anywhere

Number of players: Four to twelve

Materials: None

The traditional English Christmas song was originally a memory game and was brought to the United States by English settlers. Players sit in a circle, and the first player begins by saying: "On the first day of Christmas, my true love brought to me, one . . . ," then adds the name of a bird, such as a dove.

The second player continues: "On the second day of Christmas, my true love brought to me, one dove, two . . . ," adding the name of another bird, and so on.

A player who forgets the name of a bird or repeats them out of order has to give a forfeit, to be redeemed after the end of the game (see Forfeits, page 19). The game continues until only one player is left, and that player is in charge of assigning forfeits.

In a version of this game from England, players not only have to remember the correct words, but they must say the entire list without taking a breath.

For more information about memory games and a list of other memory games in this book, see page 30.

Native American—Apache
Jackstones

Playing area: A clear space on the ground or floor, indoors or outdoors

Number of players: Two or more

Materials: Five small stones

In one jackstone game, the "rock game," a player scatters four stones. She places her nonthrowing hand flat on the ground, palm downward, and tosses the fifth stone up into the air with the other. With each toss, she picks up one of the four stones, places it on one of the knuckles of her other hand, and then catches the tossed stone before it hits the ground.

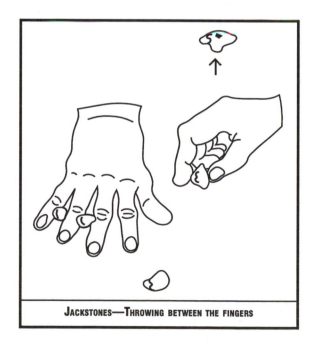

JACKSTONES—THROWING BETWEEN THE FINGERS

A more difficult game is called "throwing between the fingers." The player places one hand on the ground, palm downward. He scatters four stones on the ground and tosses the fifth in the air as he picks up the other stones, one at a time, and places them so that they are gripped between the fingers of the other hand. Then he turns that hand over, and tossing the fifth stone in the air, removes the stones one by one from between his fingers and places them on the ground.

For more information about jacks games and a list of other jacks games in this book, see page 26.

Marbles

Playing area: A smooth, level, dirt area

Number of players: Four (two teams of two)

Materials: Twenty or more marbles for each team

Before manufactured marbles were available to them, Apache children rolled marbles from clay, then dried them in the sun or by the fire. They also used small round stones.

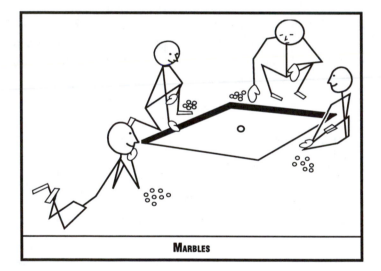

MARBLES

For this game, there are two players on each team, and team members sit across from each other around a shallow square scooped out of the dirt. One player places a marble in the center of the square, and an opposing player attempts to hit it with one of his marbles. If he succeeds, his team collects both marbles, and the other team must place another marble in the center of the square. When a player misses, his team must substitute one of their marbles for the one in the center, which is given to the other team.

The object of this game is to hit an opponent's marble (unlike other marble games in which the opponent's marble must be knocked completely out of a circle). To assure a challenging game, players should adjust the size of the playing square to their skills.

For more information about marbles and a list of other marbles games in this book, see page 29.

Native American—Arapahoe
Ring and Pin

Playing area: Indoors or outdoors

Number of players: Two or more

Materials: Traditional materials for making a ring and pin are a long, bone needle, a length of thin cord, and several cross-sections of deer leg bone. Today, players can make a ring-and-pin from a pencil, a shoelace, and four one-inch sections of a cardboard tube (from a roll of foil or plastic wrap).

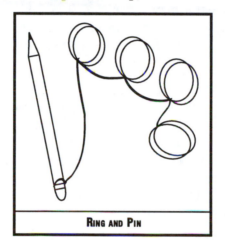

RING AND PIN

To make a ring and pin, a player ties the shoelace to the eraser end of the pencil. This will be the bottom end of the ring and pin. Then she ties the first ring at a distance from the pencil of one pencil-length plus one-quarter inch. The distance between the other rings should be one inch.

According to the Arapahoe game rules, a player receives points for spearing a ring, beginning with the one nearest the pencil, as follows: two, three, four, and five points. If several rings are caught at once, the point value is equal to the total number of rings, not the total of the values of each. Each player keeps a running score of her points and continues to play until she misses or has tried for an agreed-upon number of times. Then the play passes to another player.

The ring-and-pin game has been widely played by many tribes throughout North America. The materials used to create the game vary depending on the local resources and the amount of challenge desired by the players. The Walapai played the game with a mesquite stick and a rabbit skull. A sinew was tied through the nose holes of the skull, and the other end was attached to the stick. Players scored different numbers of points depending upon which hole in the skull the stick went through when it was caught, a smaller hole counting more than a larger one. Salmon-fishing tribes such as the Hupa, Yurok, and the Shasta used a slender pin and rings made of fish vertebrae. The Mohave used rings cut from the skin of a dried gourd.

Native American—Chippewa
Moccasin Game

Playing area: A space, indoors or outdoors, where players can sit comfortably on the ground

Number of players: Two teams of two to six players each

Materials: Four moccasins (hats or squares of cloth, which are both traditional, are easier for children to use); four small objects such as pebbles or marbles, one of which is a different color than the others; twenty-four counting sticks for each team

The players are divided into two equal teams, then sit across from one another. Between them on the ground are four moccasins, hats, or squares of cloth. The first player from one team places an object under each moccasin, trying not to let the other team see where each object is placed. Then the first player of the other team guesses where the object of a different color is hidden. The guesser is awarded four points if he guesses correctly on his first try, three points if correct on the second try, and two points if correct on the third try, and it becomes his turn to hide the objects. If, however, the player cannot find the object on the third try, the first team hides the objects again, and the second player on the opposing team guesses where they are. Counting sticks are given by one team to the other according to the number of points scored by each guesser. The team that claims all of the other team's counting sticks wins the game.

Singing was traditionally an important part of the moccasin game. A team would sing as the objects were being hidden and would continue singing until the object was found.

Similar hiding games were widespread among Native North American tribes. Although they are primarily adult games, children would watch from the sidelines, then imitate the play themselves.

For more information about guessing games and a list of other guessing games in this book, see page 20.

Native American—Comanche
Grizzly Bear

Playing area: A medium-sized, open space

Number of players: Five to fifteen

Materials: A small pile of sand or gravel (about a bucketful); chalk for drawing a circle if playing on pavement or sidewalk

Players make a pile of sand in the middle of the playing area and draw a circle around it, about five or six feet across. One player is chosen as the grizzly bear, and another as the mother. These two roles should be taken by two of the oldest players. The rest of the players are the children, and they line up behind their mother and hold onto each other's shoulders or waists. The mother protects her young from the grizzly bear. The bear tries to tag the last child in line, and when he succeeds, the line breaks up and all the children try to take the bear's "sugar" represented by the pile of sand. The bear goes to his circle, and must keep his feet inside the line (though he is allowed to reach outside the circle to grab the children). The children take as much sugar as they can without being tagged by the bear. Each child tagged is tickled by the bear and is "caught." The game continues until all the children are caught or until all the sugar is taken.

For more information about tag and chasing games and a list of other line tag and guarding the treasure games in this book, see page 35.

For more information about tag and chasing games and a list of other line tag and guarding the treasure games in this book, see page 35.

Native American—Crow
Icbirikyu

Playing area: The shore of a lake, stream, or river

Number of players: Any number

Materials: Stones

Each player in turn tosses a stone high up into the air and repeats the words "*Icbirikyu babirikyup*" over and over until the stone hits the water. A player wins if the stone splashes down at exactly the same time that she finishes saying "*babirikyup*." These words are apparently nonsense words that are used only in this game.

Native American—Inuit
Ducks and Ptarmigans

Playing area: A large, clear, outdoor space with a soft surface

Number of players: Two even teams and a starter

Materials: A rope long enough for all the players to hold

This tug-of-war game has been used to foretell the coming season's weather. The game is traditionally played in the fall of the year, with both adults and children participating. Players divide into two teams, the ptarmigans and the ducks. Ptarmigans are birds that stay in the Arctic during the winter, while ducks fly south.

167

Players born in the winter are the "ptarmigans," while the "ducks" are those born in summer. (You can use the spring and fall equinoxes as dividing points. Anyone born on the equinox can be placed on the smaller team.) The teams pull on a long rope (traditionally made of sealskin in Alaska). They draw a line on the ground and make a mark at the center of the rope. The two teams line up on either side of the rope, and at a signal, they begin to pull. If the ducks succeed in dragging all the ptarmigans across the line, the coming winter will be mild, but if the ptarmigans win, the winter will be cold.

For more information about tug-of-war games, see page 39.

Native American—Jicarilla Apache
*Raven Goes to His Child

Playing area: A medium-sized space, indoors or outdoors, with lots of hiding places

Number of players: Five to thirty

Materials: A small object that will be hidden

Players decide on the boundaries of the playing area, and one of them is chosen to be It. The others show It an object. Then It closes his eyes, and someone hides the object. It uncovers his eyes and must find the hidden object, which is called the "raven's egg." When It is close to the hidden object all the other players clap their hands and cry out "caw, caw, caw," imitating a raven's behavior of flapping wings and calling out when someone comes near its nest. If It gets further away from the raven's egg, the other players' "caw, caw, caw" becomes softer. After the child finds the object, another player takes his place.

For more information about hide-and-seek and a list of other hidden object games in this book, see page 23.

Native American—Kwakiutl
Quaquatsewa-iu
(Stick Drop)

Playing space: Anywhere

Number of players: Two to ten

Materials: A bundle of small sticks (pick-up sticks or straws will do); a stronger stick just an inch or two longer, with a ring attached to the top end, parallel to the ground (like a basketball hoop). (The ring should be just a bit bigger in circumference than that of the amount of sticks or straws that a player can grasp in one hand.)

QUAQUATSEWA-IU (STICK DROP)

A player places the stick with the ring firmly in the ground, or one player holds it at ground level. Each player takes the bundle of sticks in one hand, holds that hand directly above the hoop, and lets the sticks fall, trying to make as many as possible fall into the ring. The game is made even more challenging by blindfolding the players, or by blindfolding them and spinning them around before they drop the sticks through the ring.

Traditionally, the stick with the hoop is 16 inches long and stuck in the ground. The sticks in the bundle held over the hoop are a little longer than the distance from a player's hand to the hoop.

For more information about target games and a list of other target games in this book, see page 38.

Native American—Makah
Shuttlecock

Playing area: Indoors or outdoors

Number of players: Two to ten

Materials: A paddle and shuttlecock for each player (or players can take turns using one or two sets)

When playing this game, the Makah used paddles made from a thin cross-section of a cedar log. Ping-pong paddles, wooden plates, or any similar round, unbreakable disk also work well.

The Makah made the shuttlecock from a short, wood cylinder cut from a branch, with three feathers tied at one end and held in place with pine pitch. A similar shuttlecock can be made from a bottle cork and three feathers, each about four inches long. Place the feathers around the outer edge of the cork and secure them with white glue, then wrap and tie string around the cork to keep the feathers in place.

Players compete to see which one can hit the shuttlecock into the air with the paddle the most times without letting the shuttlecock touch the ground.

For more information about shuttlecock games and a list of other shuttlecock games in this book, see page 32.

Native American—Nootka
Laughing Games

Playing area: The beach or other sandy area

Number of players: Two for *Tsumh*; two teams of three or more for *No'awa*

Materials: None for *Tsumh*; a thin stick about two feet long for *No'awa*

Tsumh. To signal the beginning of a game, someone shouts *"Tsumh!"* Everyone stands completely still, staring at each other, with no expression on their faces. The first to smile or laugh loses the game.

No'awa. One team pushes a stick into the sand on a beach and lines up behind it. The first player in line kneels behind the stick. They sing a song, then call the name of a player on the other team. That player must walk toward them very slowly and lift the stick out of the sand, all with a serious expression on her face. The team members "defending the stick" do everything they can to make her smile or laugh. If the player does smile or laugh, another player from her team is called. When someone from the opposing team finally succeeds in taking the stick without smiling or laughing, he sets it up on his team's side of the playing area and calls one of the opposite team to come forward.

This game could be adapted for other environments, and another object could be substituted for the stick.

For other laughing games, see Syria: Don't Laugh and United States: The Prince of Morocco.

Native American—Omaha
Dua

Playing area: Indoors or outdoors

Number of players: Two to ten

Materials: A stick, three to four feet long

Players mark the playing stick with a series of small notches from end to end. The object is for a player to touch each notch, saying *"dua"* each time he does so. The player who touches the greatest number of notches on a single breath, saying *dua* all the while, is the winnner.

The Nootka (Canada) have played a similar game called *Pin'an,* which is also a test of breath holding. Children find a very long frond of bracken fern and remove every other branch from the stalk. Children then take turns holding the frond and touching each tiny branchlet with their fingers, moving down the stalk, saying *"pina"* each time. The child who moves the farthest down the stalk before taking a breath wins.

See a similar game in this book from Zaire, *Bokwele.*

Native American—Pamunkey
Hide-and-Switch

Playing area: Outdoors or a large indoor space with plenty of places to hide a small object

Number of players: Five or more

Materials: A stick about four inches long

The players agree upon the boundaries of the game, within which the stick may be hidden. They also agree on the location of a home base, such as a tree. One player hides the stick while the others cover their eyes. That player, who will not take part in the game, lets the others know when to uncover their eyes. They look for the stick, and the one who finds it chases the others, trying to tag them with it before they reach the safety of the home base. The player who found the stick hides it, and the game begins again.

In the Pamunkey game, the player who found the stick would try to switch the others with it. This is the reason the game is called Hide-and-Switch.

For more information about hide-and-seek games and a list of other hidden object games in this book, see page 23.

Native American—Pima
Gins
(Sticks)

Playing area: A flat, clear, dirt or sand area

Number of players: Two (or two teams)

Materials: Four flat sticks, about six inches long and one inch wide, marked on one

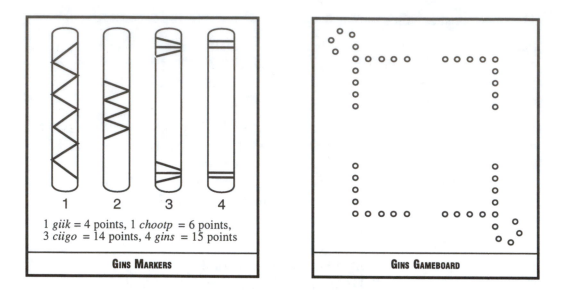

1 *giik* = 4 points, 1 *chootp* = 6 points,
3 *ciigo* = 14 points, 4 *gins* = 15 points

GINS MARKERS

GINS GAMEBOARD

side as in the illustration; a flat stone and a short marking stick for each player or team

In this game, four sticks are thrown, and the way they land determines the number of spaces a player can move his marker. Designs are marked on one side only of each stick, as in the illustration. A rectangle is marked in the dirt as the playing area, and small holes are dug into it as marked. In the traditional Pima game, the rectangle is quite large, about nine by 13 feet. The two semicircles of five holes each at the opposing corners are called "houses" and are the starting places for each player. Players each put a stick, called *ginse* (the horse), into the outermost hole of their houses.

The traditional way to throw the sticks, or dice, is as follows: hold them loosely in the right hand, tilt them slightly forward, and hit the bottoms of them with a flat rock held in the left hand. Each player uses his own rock. After they fall on the ground, the score is counted as follows:

> *giik*—4 points
> *chootp*—6 points
> *ciigo*—14 points
> *gins*—15 points

These values are used when only one stick lands with the patterned side up. Other-wise the score is:

> Two patterned sides up—2 points
> Three patterned sides up—3 points
> Four patterned sides up—5 points
> All unmarked sides up—10 points

After each throw, the player who threw the sticks adds up his score and moves accordingly. The player moves his horse (marker) first along the holes of his house, then on around the square. Anytime a player throws the same number as the previous player, the horse of the player making the second throw is "killed," and he must begin again in the first square of the house. Whenever a player's horse lands in a hole occupied by the other horse, the other horse must return to his house and start over. Passing over another horse does no harm. After a horse has traveled all the way around the square, it must reverse and return to the first hole of the house. His object is *not* to throw the exact number needed to arrive at the last hole, because if he does, he is "in the fire" and cannot win until he throws either a 14 or a 15.

For more information about board games and a list of other board games in this book, see page 14. For more information about dice, knucklebones, and games of chances and a list of other games of chance in this book, see page 17.

Wee-ichida
(Racing Game)

Playing area: A large, open field or a circular track

Number of players: Two

Materials: A ball for each player

The traditional kicking ball of the Pima is a lightweight volcanic rock or wooden ball, around two and a half inches in diameter, covered with the gum or pitch from a plant such as mesquite. Players can make a similar ball by purchasing a wood ball, two inches in diameter, from a craft store and covering it with a layer of wide rubber bands.

As they race around the course, players kick the ball with a lifting and throwing motion, rather than a hard kick with the toes. It is important, of course, not to lose the ball. Some Pima players were rumored to cheat by carrying extra balls with them.

Ball races have long been an important ceremonial sport among Native peoples of the areas of the southwestern United States and northwestern Mexico. Sometimes Pima runners would run these ball races for eight to 10 miles. Some ball races, such as those of the Tarahumara of Mexico, were run by teams, all kicking one ball.

For more information about racing games and a list of other racing games in this book, see page 31.

Native American—Shawnee
Tetepaulalowaawaa
(Rolling Game)

Playing area: A clear area of hard dirt, about four feet wide and fifteen to twenty feet long

Number of players: Two, or two teams

Materials: An equal number of marbles for each player or team

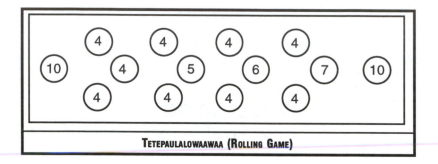

TETEPAULALOWAAWAA (ROLLING GAME)

In this game, players roll marbles or small stone or wood balls down a track into pits scooped out of the earth. Players or teams take turns rolling one marble, and score points as in the illustration.

For more information about marbles and a list of other marbles games in this book, see page 29.

Native American—Sioux
Marbles

Playing area: A flat, smooth, ice surface

Number of players: Two equal teams of three to six players

Materials: One marble for each player, and a small, lightweight wood block (about two inches by two inches by four inches)

The teams sit opposite each another, about 50 feet apart, with the wood block set on its short edge at an equal distance between them. The players on one team shoot their marbles, one after another, at the block. If they succeed in knocking it over, the block is reset, and that team plays again. Whenever a team fails to knock over the wood block, all their marbles go to the opposing team, who begin shooting their marbles at the target. There is usually a wager on the game, and the winning team takes a bracelet, hair ornament, or other valuable item from the losers.

174

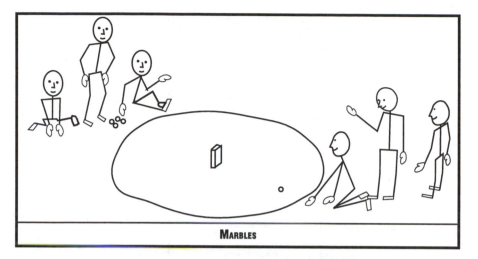

MARBLES

This game was traditionally played sitting on ice, but a hard floor could be used in an indoor setting. The Sioux used perfectly spherical rocks when they could find them. Parents also made marbles for their children out of the same red stone used in pipe-making.

For more information about marbles and a list of other marbles games in this book, see page 29.

Native American—Teton Sioux
Hoop and Pole

Playing area: A large, flat, open space outdoors

Number of players: Six or more

Materials: A hoop, sixteen to twenty inches in diameter (rattan hoops may be purchased at crafts stores); three-foot hardwood dowels as poles

Hoop-and-pole games like this one were played by Native Americans throughout most of North America north of Mexico. Players throw a pole (a spear, arrow, or dart) at a rolling hoop. In most cases, the players' objective is not to throw the pole through the hoop, but to throw the pole in such a way as to make the hoop stop. In some traditions, the hoop is wrapped with string to create a network or web in the center, and points are scored according to what part of this web was pierced by the pole.

In this version of the hoop-and-pole game, the players' goal is to stop the hoop, usually by throwing the pole in front of it as it rolls. The hoop is marked with one of the symbols in the illustration at each of the four quarter-points. To score, a player's spear must be touching the hoop after it falls, and the player is awarded points according to which symbol the spear is closest to.

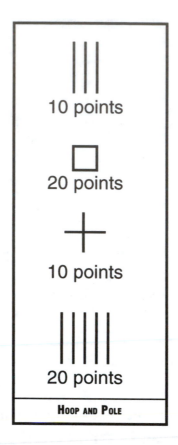

The two teams of players begin by lining up facing each other. Two extra players stand at either end of the playing area and roll the hoop back and forth. The game begins when the hoop is rolled between the lines, and a player from each team throws a pole at the hoop as it rolls.

The game can be made much safer by having both teams line up in one line along the course of the hoop, so that the two players shoot from the same side.

For more information about target games and a list of other target games in this book, see page 38.

Native American—Winnebago
Hahi'bidjikeeun
(Tree Game)

Playing area: An outdoor space with two trees twenty feet or more apart (one tree must have a large branch about ten feet above the ground)

Number of players: Five or more

Materials: A soft ball or other soft object suitable for throwing at the players

The tree branch is the first target in this throw-and-tag game. One player is chosen as It. All the other players stand behind a line near the tree that has the target branch. It tries to hit the tree branch with the ball. She keeps trying until she succeeds. As soon as the ball hits the limb, all the players run to the other tree, and they are safe as soon as they touch it. It retrieves the ball as quickly as she can, then throws it at one of the runners. If she fails to hit another player before he reaches the safety of the other tree, she must be It again. If she does hit someone, that player becomes It for the next game.

For more information about tag and chasing games and a list of other tag and chasing games in this book, see page 37. For more information about ball games and a list of other ball games in this book, see page 12.

Native American—Yupik
Uhl-ta
(Ring Around)

Playing area: A large, clear, outdoor space

Number of players: Two equal teams of four or more

Materials: None

This is a team race. Players mark start and finish lines, at least 20 or 30 feet apart. Players hold hands and form a circle, facing toward the center. Each team stands entirely behind the starting line. When a starting signal is given, both teams begin to circle around and at the same time move toward the finish line. The first team to completely cross the finish line while still holding hands is the winner.

For more information about racing games and a list of other racing games in this book, see page 31.

Native American—Zuni
Kolowis Awithlaknannai
(Fighting Serpents)

Playing area: Anywhere

Number of players: Two

Materials: Any flat surface on which to draw the game board; twenty-three markers for each player

Players draw the diagram on a flat surface, then place the markers on the board as shown. The object of the game is for one player to capture all the markers of the opposing player.

The first player moves one of his markers onto one of the three vacant points. Players then take turns moving along a line to an adjacent point. Players must move their

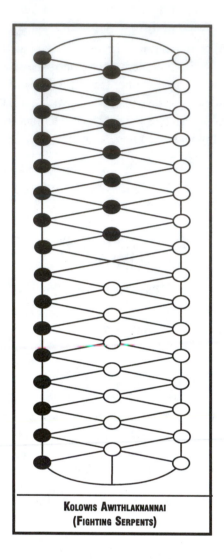

**KOLOWIS AWITHLAKNANNAI
(FIGHTING SERPENTS)**

pieces along a straight line—going around the curved end of the board is not allowed. They capture each other's markers by jumping over them whenever possible. Markers are removed from the board when captured. They may capture more than one marker at a time with successive jumps. The game ends when one player has lost all his markers.

The Zuni game is probably based on an Alquerque type of game introduced by the Spanish in the sixteenth century. The name of this game, *Kolowis Awithlaknannai,* comes from the name of a mythical serpent (*Kolowis*) and the word for "stones kill" (*Awithlaknannai*).

For more information about board games and a list of other board games in this book, see page 14.

*Tsi-ko-na
(Ring Toss)

Playing area: A medium-sized, clear space, indoors or outdoors

Number of players: Two

Materials: Two rings, one about four inches in diameter, the other about three inches in diameter

One player begins the game by tossing the large ring to the ground. The second player stands at the same place and tosses her ring, aiming it inside the larger ring. The first player, who is throwing the larger ring, continues throwing until the other player succeeds in placing the small ring inside it. Then the two trade roles.

This game can be made easier for young children by using rings with a greater size difference.

For more information about target games and a list of other target games in this book, see page 38.

Native Hawaiian
Kimokimo

Playing area: A flat, clear space on floor, dirt, or pavement

Number of players: Two or more

Materials: Ten or more pebbles for each player

This is a game like jacks, but played with pebbles. Each player chooses one pebble for tossing, and the rest are placed in one pile on the ground. The players sit in a tight circle. The first player tosses her pebble, called the *kimo,* and picks up a stone from the pile of *ai,* or food, with the same hand, and then catches the *kimo,* continuing until she misses. Then the next player takes a turn, and so on until the pile is gone. The player with the most *ai* is the winner.

A nearly identical game, *Timotimo*, is played in Tahiti.

For more information about jacks games and a list of other jacks games in this book, see page 26.

Puerto Rico
Por Aqui Hay Candela
(Here Is a Light)

Playing area: A medium-sized, clear space, indoors or outdoors

Number of players: Ten to twenty-five

Materials: None

Players form a circle. To be sure they are spaced evenly around the circle, they hold up their arms and touch fingertips with the players on either side. One player is chosen to be It. It goes from one player to the next, saying, "Give me a light from your fire."

The player replies, "The fire is over there," and points to another player (or says that person's name). The player who is It must go and ask that player for fire. In the meantime, players in the circle are changing places with one another. It tries to run quickly and take one of the empty places, but is not allowed to run while she is talking to one of the players—she must try to grab a spot for herself in between questions and answers. When she does find a place, the player who is left out becomes It.

For more information about tag and chasing games and a list of other exchanging places games in this book, see page 36.

Man-tan-tiru-liru-lá

Playing area: A medium-sized space, indoors or outdoors

Number of players: Five to ten

Materials: None

Man-tan-tiru-liru-lá is a nonsense word. All the players will have to practice it until they can say it easily, because they will be repeating it often during the game. Every line in this dramatic game ends with *man-tan-tiru-liru-lá,* which makes the game much more fun.

One player is the boss, and the others are workers. The boss proposes various occupations to the workers, and they refuse one or more jobs, giving reasons why (the cleverer the better) until the boss offers a job they will accept. This game is played for the joy of invention and word-play, and also provides an opportunity for children to think about different jobs.

A dialogue between the boss and a worker might go like this:

Boss: I am looking for a worker *man-tan-tiru-liru-lá.*

All Workers: Which one of us do you want *man-tan-tiru-liru-lá?*

Boss: I want (so-and-so) *man-tan-tiru-liru-lá.*

Worker: What job do you want me to do *man-tan-tiru-liru-lá?*

Boss: I am looking for a gardener *man-tan-tiru-liru-lá.*

Worker: I don't want to be a gardener. I'll get too dirty (or "I might turn green," or "Flowers make me sneeze") *man-tan-tiru-liru-lá.*

All Workers: He doesn't want to be a gardener. He'll get too dirty *man-tan-tiru-liru-lá.*

The boss keeps proposing jobs and the worker making excuses, until finally a job is offered that appeals to him.

For more information about drama and pantomime games and a list of other miming games in this book, see page 18. For more information on storytelling and word games and a list of other storytelling and word games, see page 33.

Venezuela
Plant Market

Playing area: Indoors or outdoors

Number of players: Ten to thirty

Materials: None

One player is chosen as the seller and another as the buyer. The rest are the plants for sale. Players select one category of plant that they are familiar with—vegetables, flowers, or trees, for example. The players may choose names for themselves, or the seller can whisper the name of a plant in each one's ear. The buyer should not know what names they have chosen. The buyer comes to the market and says to the seller, "What nice vegetables you have today."

The seller replies, "Yes, I just picked them this morning." Then the buyer begins to ask for vegetables by name. Players have decided in advance how many incorrect guesses he will be allowed, such as five or seven. Whenever the buyer asks for a vegetable that is in the market, that player goes and stands behind him. When the buyer asks for a vegetable that is not in the market, the seller must invent a reason for not having it, such as, "They are not ripe yet," or "My dog ate all of them this morning."

The game ends when the buyer either gets all the vegetables or uses up his guesses. Then a new buyer and seller are chosen, and the game begins again. The goal of the game is to improvise, have fun, and amuse one another.

A game like this, called *Gartnerspiel,* is played in Germany. In Italy and Yugoslavia, the game is called Bird Market.

For more information about drama and pantomime games and a list of other market games in this book, see page 18.

Vietnam
Biting the Carp's Tail

Playing area: A large, clear, outdoor space

Number of players: Ten or more

Materials: None

A carp is a fish from the same family as the goldfish. Players form a line, each one holding onto the shoulders, waist, or clothing of the player in front. Together, they are the carp. The first person in line is the carp's head, the last one is its tail. The head tries to catch and hold the tail, and the tail tries not to get caught. The players in the middle (the more the better) have lots of fun.

This game works best with a very large, mixed-age group. It is also played in China and Thailand. The creature formed by the line of players is called either a dragon or a fish. In a similar game from Germany, *Teufelsschwanz,* the head must catch the tail before a song has been sung three times. Games like this have also been recorded in New Hebrides, France, and the Netherlands.

For more information about tag and chasing games and a list of other tag and chasing games in this book, see page 37.

Yemen
Name Tag

Playing area: A medium-sized, clear space with established boundaries, indoors or outdoors

Number of players: Six or more

Materials: A blindfold

One player is chosen to be It and is blindfolded. All the others try to avoid being tagged, but must not go outside the boundaries of the playing area. Whenever It calls the name of a player, that player must answer "Yes" or "Here I am." The first player caught becomes It.

For more information about blindfold games and a list of other blindfold games in this book, see page 13.

Zaire
Bokwele

Playing area: A medium-sized space, indoors or outdoors

Number of players: Equal teams of four or more players each

Materials: For each team, a long pole

182

The poles used to play this game should be eight to 10 feet long or longer, depending on players' ability to hold their breath. The poles should be thin enough that the players can encircle them with one hand. Lengths of heavy rope or tubing could be substituted for the poles.

Players begin holding one end on the pole, then go hand over hand while constantly repeating, *"Bokwele."* Their hands must touch each other at every grasp, and they must not take a breath or stop repeating the word. Each player who makes it from one end of the pole to the other on one breath, saying *"Bokwele"* the entire time, scores a point for that team.

For a similar game, see the Native American—Omaha game *Dua* on page 170.

Zambia
Hand-Clapping Game

Playing area: Space for two lines of players, standing facing each other
Number of players: Ten to twenty, including one or two scorekeepers
Materials: None

The players divide into two equal or nearly equal teams and line up facing each other. The first two players in each line are the leaders. They play the game until one leader loses and moves to the end of the line. Then the next player takes that one's place, and the game begins again.

The two leaders face each other and hold both arms up in the air. The first leader brings his hands down, and all the players clap three times rhythmically. On the next beat, the leader puts one hand out, palm forward, as in most hand-clapping games. The other player must clap at exactly the same time and put out the same hand (right to right or left to left) so that the two hands meet. If the second player puts out the opposite hand, he is "wounded" and must go to the end of the line. If the second player puts up the correct hand, the leader is "wounded" and must go to the end of the line. The other player then becomes the leader. Anyone wounded three times is dead and must drop out of the game entirely. A tally of the number of losses by each team is kept, and the team with the fewest losses after a given amount of times wins the game.

For more information about guessing games and a list of other gesture anticipation games in this book, see page 21.

Zimbabwe
*Kanzhinge

Playing area: A large, clear, outdoor space

Number of players: Eight to fifteen

Materials: None

Two players join their upraised hands and form a bridge, while the others line up and pass under the bridge, singing, *"Banangu bamanina mukasaka kazhinge,"* which means "My children circle through the forest."

Each time the line passes under the bridge, the players forming the bridge trap the last one, who takes a place behind one or the other of them, until only one player is left. This last player uses all his guile and speed to get under the bridge without being caught. As he runs under the bridge he sings, *"Kanga kazhinge kaladikumbakumba mu twembezhi,"* which means "The little, little quail scratches among the herd-boys."

The others answer, *"Kaladikumba"* or "It scratches about."

The last player continues to run through the bridge until he, too, is caught.

For more information about London Bridge games and a list of other London Bridge games in this book, see page 28.

Whistling Race

Playing area: Outdoors on a long path or sidewalk

Number of players: Three or more

Materials: Chalk or sticks to mark on the ground

Players mark a starting line on a path or sidewalk. A player begins running and whistling at exactly the same time, and another player jogs alongside her. The runner must stop when she stops whistling, and the spot where she has stopped is marked by the player who has accompanied her. The winner is the player who can jog the farthest on one whistling breath.

For more information about racing games and a list of other racing games in this book, see page 31.

PART 3
Games and Teaching

Chapter 4
Collecting and Exploring Traditional Games

The study of traditional games is an excellent cross-cultural project for an elementary school class. Traditional games reveal the ways in which people of different cultures are alike. They show that children all over the world play the same kinds of games and find the same types of activities enjoyable. Through traditional games, an educator can lead children to make these and other discoveries for themselves.

Another good reason for studying traditional games is that nearly all students have some firsthand knowledge of the subject. Traditional games are not found only in some cultures. All children, and their families, have some unique and interesting traditional games to share. As a result, students will participate eagerly in class discussions about traditional games.

Students' interest in self-directed projects based on traditional games can be sustained for days and even weeks. Some research on traditional games can be done in the library and much more information can be gathered by interviewing friends, family, and people in the community, an activity many students enjoy immensely.

While participating in projects such as those outlined on the following pages, students will have opportunities to develop useful skills, such as oral communication, operating audio and video recorders, using a computer database program, and creating displays and publications. Many of the following projects require what folklorists refer to as field research, in which they decide on an activity they want to know more about, locate people who are or have been engaged in that activity, and interview them. Field researchers observe behavior and collect materials. Just as a geologist collects rock samples or a paleontologist collects fossils, a folklorist collects folklore, including traditional games.

Because games are activities, not physical objects, a field researcher collects them by making some type of record; for example, she can write down the rules of a game, and draw pictures or take photographs of where and how and with what materials games are played. She can publish her findings in books, and store photos and recordings in archives. A videotape is often the best way to capture the actions of a game. However, if a game exists only in a person's memory, a field researcher can tape record that person's description of the game and transcribe the description later or take written notes.

The collecting methods you and your group choose will depend upon the age of the students, the availability of recording equipment, and the ways in which you intend to display, share, and store the results of your field research.

Before you begin any of the following projects, it is a good idea to try to recall the traditional games you played as a child. Read about some of the games types in Chapter 2 to stimulate your memory. Also, take time to observe the students you will be working with during their free play, and try to identify the games they are playing. Later, you will be able to suggest those games as examples during class discussions.

INTRODUCING TRADITIONAL GAMES TO GRADES K–2

Lesson Plan 1: Baby Games

In this lesson, children learn to identify traditional games, and recall and describe some from their own experience.

Almost all families play games with babies. Adults and older brothers and sisters sing songs as they clap hands and sometimes tickle the baby. These may not seem to be traditional games at first, especially because the baby does not really play voluntarily. However, they are patterned behaviors that include traditional rhymes, they are not learned from books, and the rules are negotiable.

For this lesson, find a doll or stuffed animal about the size of a one-year-old child. The doll or animal should have fingers and toes, since digits play an important role in many baby games. Practice some baby games that you remember. "This Little Piggy Went to Market" and "Pat-a-Cake" are examples from English-speaking tradition. Using the doll, demonstrate one or two baby games to your students, then ask them to share any baby games they know. Pass the doll around so that students who know baby games can demonstrate them. Then choose one or two of the games that have been shared and learn them as a group.

Ask the children why they think families play games with a baby. Some possibilities are:

- Babies giggle and everyone feels good

- Babies can not really have conversations, so this is an enjoyable way to spend time with them

- Baby games exercise babies' muscles

- Baby games help babies learn language

Lesson Plan 2: Recalling Traditional Games

Introduce the term "traditional game," and provide some examples of traditional games you played as a child or that you have seen students playing. Offer simple guidelines for identifying traditional games, such as the following:

- Kids learn traditional games from other kids

- Kids decide when and where to play traditional games

- The rules of traditional games do not need to be written down because everyone remembers them

- Traditional games are not bought at the store (or, if store-bought objects, such as jacks, marbles, or a jump rope, are used to play a traditional game, they are inexpensive)

Ask the students to think of traditional games that they play with friends. Some possibilities are jacks, jump rope, hand clapping, and hide-and-seek. Make a list on the board of the games they suggest, and test each game against the guidelines above. Remember that the distinctions between traditional games, manufactured games, and organized sports are somewhat fluid. For example, marbles can be played in traditional or folk ways and by official, regulation rules. If you cannot decide whether a certain game is a traditional game, put it into a separate category of games, "not yet classified."

Lesson Plan 3: Games Collecting Assignment

After the introductory exploration of traditional games in the previous lessons, many children will be ready to interview a family member or neighbor and collect a traditional game from that person's childhood. Have the students decide as a group on one or two game types that they will try to find. Some fruitful game types for this assignment are hopscotch, marbles, jacks, hide-and-seek, and tag. Students may need to interview more than one person before they find someone who played a game of the chosen type as a child.

Depending upon the ages and abilities of the students, have them present the results of their field research to the class orally or in writing. If they are too young to take notes, have them ask their interviewee to draw a simple picture or diagram showing how the game was played. The child can use this as a memory aid when reporting orally to the class.

INTRODUCING TRADITIONAL GAMES TO GRADES 3–6

Lesson Plan 1: Traditional Games, Purchased Games, and Organized Sports

In this lesson, students learn to distinguish between traditional games, purchased games, and organized sports. Begin by introducing some of the characteristics of traditional games from page 4. You can simplify these somewhat. We find that children catch on quickly to the concept if we tell them that these are games that:

- Kids learn traditional games from other kids

- Kids decide when and where to play traditional games

- The rules of traditional games do not need to be written down because everyone remembers them

- Traditional games are not bought at the store (or, if store-bought objects, such as jacks, marbles, or a jump rope, are used to play a traditional game, they are inexpensive)

The students will no doubt enjoy hearing you describe the traditional games that you played as a child.

Ask the students what tradional games they play or played when they were younger, and list these games on the board. Decide whether the games meet the criteria above, and move any that do not to either the "purchased games" or "organized sports" category. There will probably be games that you cannot decide how to categorize. For instance, in the United States jumping rope is both a traditional game played on the street and a competitive organized sport. Basketball is an organized sport, but most pickup games played with a basketball and one hoop have the characteristics of traditional games.

Discuss how the traditional games on your list differ from purchased board games, video games, and team sports, listing positive and negative things about each type of game. When might students choose to play a traditional game rather than one of the other types?

Lesson Plan 2: Stability and Variation in Traditional Games

Select a game that most students have played. Two games that usually bring a broad response are Hide-and-Seek and Scissors-Paper-Stone. These games, or ones like them, are also played by children in many cultures.

After your group has agreed upon a game, ask students to write answers to the following questions about the game and then to compare notes in small groups prior to a whole-group discussion:

190

- How do you play the game? (What are the rules?)

- Are there any special motions, words, or phrases you use when you play?

- What makes a good player?

- What happens to the winner? The loser?

This exercise should show students that there are striking similarities, as well as interesting differences, in the ways they play the game. Next pose the question, "How can this be the same game when different people play by different rules?" The answer is, it is a traditional game. Traditional games have stability (they stay pretty much the same) and variation (they are played with many minor variations). Can the students think of anything else they or their families do that have stability and variation? Birthday and holiday celebrations are an obvious example. Stability and variation, across both time and space, are characteristics of nearly every kind of traditional folklore activity.

TRADITIONAL GAMES COLLECTING PROJECT FOR GRADES 3–6

Lesson Plan: What Did You Do When You Were a Kid?

In this project, the teacher will ask students to interview someone in the community about the traditional games that person played as a child. The following is a sequence of steps that can be included in the project:

1. Decide how the results of the field research will be presented (orally or written, for example).

2. Have each student identify several people they could interview. The interviewees need not be elders. College-age adults make excellent interview subjects, as well.

3. Have the students develop a few sample questions. Explain that "Did you play any traditional games when you were a kid?" is probably not a good first question, since most people do not think of the games they played as traditional games, but simply as games. Try including some specific examples in the questions, for example, "When you were a kid, did you play any street games like jump rope or marbles or hopscotch?" Be sure to add a follow-up question that will allow the interview subject to describe other traditional games as well.

4. Help students decide what to take to the interview. Explain that no one can write fast enough to record speech, and some valuable information may not be spoken at all, but may come in the form of hand gestures, facial expressions, and acting out. Therefore, folklorists and anthropologists always try to record interviews on audio or videotape. If students have access to tape

recorders and video cameras, have them record the interview. Every student should at least take written notes of their interviews. Results will be most accurate if two or more students conduct the interview, and all take notes.

5. Provide time for students to practice interviewing each other while using recording equipment and/or taking notes.

Suggested preparatory reading for students

Ferretti, Fred. *The Great American Book of Sidewalk, Stoop, Dirt, Curb, and Alley Games*. New York: Workman, 1975.

This is an easy-to-read collection of traditional games from the United States. The descriptions of games are clear, short, and well illustrated.

Gallagher, Rachel. *Games in the Street*. New York: Four Winds, 1976.

This book includes many photographs and should be required background reading if your students' interview subjects were in elementary school in the 1960s or 1970s.

Page, Linda Garland, and Smith, Hilton, eds. *Foxfire Book of Toys and Games*. New York: Dutton, 1985.

Elders recall the children's traditional games of Appalachia in this book. The book is illustrated with many photographs. The authentic flavor of the interviews is a result of careful recording and transcription of interviews by field researchers.

Sturmer, Fred, and Seltzer, Adolph. *What Did You Do When You Were a Kid?* New York: St. Martin's, 1973.

This is an account of traditional games played on city streets in the United States in the 1930s. Elementary school students will appreciate the lively writing, large print, and funny cartoon illustrations.

TWELVE CLASSROOM PROJECTS FOR GRADES 3–6

Classroom Project 1: Group Research Project

Make photocopies of one the games from the "Games Treasury." Divide the class into several groups, and have each group recreate the same game. Teachers of grades three and four may choose to explain the games to the students rather than have them read the directions.

Students should be encouraged to explore the possibilities of a traditional game and to maintain a balance between being faithful to the description of the game (stability) and tinkering with the rules, if necessary, to make the game work for them (variation).

After the groups have played a game several times, bring them together to compare their experiences, asking:

- What changes did you make to the game and why?
- When and where and with what type of group do you think this game would be most fun?
- Is this game like any other games you have played?

The following are suggested games to use for this project:

Grades 3–4:

Pantomime Games:

PAKISTAN: *MAZDOORI*

RUSSIA: CZAR AND PEASANTS

TANZANIA: GIANT'S HOUSE

UNITED STATES: LEMONADE

Grades 4–5:

Changing Places Games:

AUSTRIA: NUMBERS TAG

DENMARK: THE OCEAN IS STORMY

SWEDEN: NUMBERS TAG

TURKEY: HOW DO YOU LIKE YOUR NEIGHBOR?

Grades 5–6:

Board Games:

IVORY COAST: *AWELE*

MEXICO (NATIVE TARASCAN): *EL COYOTE*

SRI LANKA: COWS AND LEOPARDS

SUDAN: *DALA*

Classroom Project 2: The Museum of Traditional Games

Establish a Museum of Children's Traditional Games in the classroom or library. Most museums contain artifacts, of course, so students will probably want to collect and display objects that are used in playing children's traditional and folk games. Drawings and photographs can also be a part of the museum collection. These can be borrowed, or students can make replicas of them using the instructions in the books listed below. You can even have the class establish a Folklore Society to work on museum displays and lead tours for parents and other students.

Resources

Botermans, Jack, et al., eds. *The World of Games: Their Origins and History, How to Play Them and How to Make Them.* New York: Facts on File, 1987.

Joseph, Joan. *Folk Toys around the World and How to Make Them.* New York: Parents' Magazine Press, 1972.

Classroom Project 3: A Traditional Games Calendar

Have students select a game from the "Games Treasury" that would be appropriate for a particular month of the year in your location. The game can be from any culture. References to games that were traditionally played in certain environments, such as on snow or sand, can be located by using the Index to Playing Environments.

Children have also played certain games during specific holiday seasons. (Armenia: Egg Jousting, Bulgaria: Gaping, and Russia: Egg Rolling are examples of games traditionally played at Easter.) Other games were played during certain seasons. Many parts of Southeast Asia experience rain for months on end, and during this rainy season, small indoor games such as jacks become quite popular. In Ethiopia, it was once believed that playing jacks would keep the rain from falling, so children were not permitted to play during the dry season.

To illustrate the games calendar, students can pose as players of each game and take photographs, or they can draw illustrations that show children playing the games. A description of how the game is played should be included on the calendar as well.

Resources

Botermans, Jack, et al., eds. *The World of Games: Their Origins and History, How to Play Them and How to Make Them.* New York: Facts on File, 1987.

This book is an excellent source of color photographs of traditional games from around the world in their cultural settings.

Daiken, Leslie. *Children's Games throughout the Year.* London: Batsford, 1949.

Old English children's games are described season by season in this collection.

Classroom Project 4: Games Bulletin Boards

Here are several ideas for ways students can display what they find out about traditional games:

- A display of traditional games collected during field research can include descriptions of games along with the personal stories that people tell about playing a game. Photographs and brief biographies of each person interviewed will make a more interesting and informative display.

- Create a traditional-games bulletin board all about the oft-dreaded role of "It." One side of the display can be about ways of choosing It, and the other can be about how it feels to be It. Assign each student to interview someone about his or her game-playing experiences. How does or did their group of friends choose It? Did they ever use any special rhymes or songs for counting out? Then ask how it feels or felt to be It. Print the results of these interviews on note cards or pieces of paper and arrange them by category on the bulletin board. Have students select a title for the bulletin board, such as "Read All About It."

- Some games have artifacts connected with them that can be displayed on a bulletin board, for instance, games that are played with paper and pencil, such as Tic Tac Toe. Pen the Pig is an American game exactly like the Afghan *Khana Baudakan* (page 44), except it is played with paper and pencil. Other traditional games are played using objects folded from paper, such as tabletop footballs and fortune tellers (also know as cootie catchers). See the resource books listed below for more examples of games played with paper and pencil.

Resources

Bronner, Simon J. *American Children's Folklore*. Little Rock, Ark.: August House, 1988.

Oakley, Ruth. *Games with Paper and Pencils*. New York: Marshall Cavendish, 1989.

Classroom Project 5: Create a Community Archive of Traditional Games

An archive is a place where important public records and documents are stored. Many public libraries keep local history archives to preserve information that has not been published in books for future researchers. Historians and writers use these archives, and so do teachers and students. If a youth group conducts interviews in the community on the subject of traditional games, it would be an excellent idea to plan a way to store the information so that it can be shared. Among the potential users of traditonal games archives are teachers looking for games from the past or games from other countries for their students to play. The information can be kept in a folder or card file, but if you put it into a computer database program, researchers will be able to access it much more easily.

A database program enables archivists to establish searchable fields as an aid to locating information. An important field in a traditional-games file would be "game type." If all hopscotch games have the word "hopscotch" typed into the game-type field, a user of the database who tells the computer that she wants to see all the hopscotch games in the file will instantly have access to them. Two fields that would be useful to teachers are the age of children who can play a certain game, and the number of children who can play. If a teacher has a group of 10 first graders, he can enter "1" into the grade field and "10" into the number of players field, and immediately find all the games in the database that his students could play as a group. Other fields that could be useful are the country or locality where the game was played, the name of the person interviewed, and the approximate year or years the game was played by the interviewee.

Classroom Project 6: Make a Video Documentary of Children's Games

All the games you need to make a great video documentary of children's traditional games are probably as close as the nearest playground. Students can videotape games and interview the players on camera, asking questions such as, "How long have you been playing this game?" "Where did you learn it?" and "Who did you learn it from?"

Fifth-grade students at Rosemont Elementary School in Los Angeles made a video of traditional games on the playground. Long, establishing shots showing a variety of games in progress were followed by close-ups that revealed the details of individual games. One student had the wonderful idea of videotaping a four-person hand-clapping game from the ground up. The camera pointed toward the sky, and the geometry and motions of the game were captured perfectly. Beginning English students at Nimitz Elementary School in Cupertino, California, videotaped each other playing games from their home countries. Most of the games included chants or songs. The students translated these into English, and a second sound track, in which they described the game, told what country it was from, and said the words of the rhyme or song in English, was added to the edited video.

The following are suggestions for creating a traditional-games videotape when you do not have editing capabilities:

- Have students preview the traditional games they might use in the video and decide which ones to include. It is best to show enough of each game that a viewer can understand how it is played from beginning to end.

- Have students make a storyboard in which they plan all of their shots in advance.

- Have them begin a game segment of the video with a close-up of a student speaking to the camera, describing what the viewers are about to see.

- Have students videotape all or part of one game.

- Close a segment with an interview of one or more of the game participants.

Classroom Project 7: Baby Games around the World

Assign your students, individually or in small groups, to collect baby games in their family or community. They may wish to use a doll or stuffed animal, as described in the lesson plan for younger children on page 188. The students should try to record the words of each game and to make simple drawings of any motions used with the game. In class, compare the different games students have collected (both the movements and the words) and discuss the ways in which these baby games are similar and/or different.

Resource

Scott, Anne. *The Laughing Baby: Remembering Nursery Rhymes and Reasons.* South Hadley, Mass.: Bergin and Garvery, 1987.

Classroom Project 8: Old Traditions Make News

Have the students write an article for the classroom or school newspaper about the class's games-collecting project. The article can include instructions and diagrams that allow the readers to re-create the games themselves.

Classroom Project 9: Create New Versions of Traditional Games

Players are always adapting traditional games to new environments and new materials. Have your class adapt some traditional game forms to their environment. Students can brainstorm for ideas, write them down, and then try them out.

New Environments. Ask them to see how many ideas they can come up with for ways to play hide-and-seek in the classroom. After students have suggested ideas and tried them out, compare them with two indoor hide-and-seek games in the "Games Treasury," *El Pan Quemado* from Paraguay (page 121) and *Sorok-sorok* from Indonesia (page 86).

Challenge students to create a version of tag that can be played in the classroom or in a family living room without disturbing anything in the room.

New Materials. Have students experiment playing some of the games in the "Games Treasury" with manufactured objects and materials (nothing natural allowed!) they find at home, in the classroom, or in the recycling bin.

Here is a list of games from the "Games Treasury" that should suggest some interesting adaptations. You may wish to make a rule that they can only use items that would otherwise be thrown away.

AUSTRALIA: JACKSTONES

BRAZIL: *PETÉCA*

CHINA: SHUTTLECOCK

JAPAN: *OTEDAMA*

LAOS: JACK STICKS

PAPUA NEW GUINEA: *TOMONG GILANG BOGL TONDIP*

THAILAND: *TAKRAW*

UGANDA: *INZAMA*

Classroom Project 10: Publish Your Own Games Book

Here are several ideas for creating books about traditional games:

- Using the *Foxfire Book of Toys and Games* or *Games in the Street* as a model, have students compile a collection of games played by class members, their families, or members of the community. Notice how the authors of the Foxfire book use photos and quotes to allow readers to get to know the individuals who played the games.

- Have students create a useful and practical book of traditional games, such as a book of baby games for new parents, or a collection of games for kids to play during "Turn Off the Television Week."

- Ask them to create a book about how one type of game is played in many different cultures. The games in the "Games Treasury" can be used as a resource. See Chapter 2 for types of games that are widely represented in the "Games Treasury." Use the books *Hopscotch around the World* and Camilla Gryski's books about string figures as examples of how such a book might look.

Resources

Gryski, Camilla. *Cat's Cradle, Owl's Eyes: A Book of String Games.* New York: William Morrow Co., 1983.

———. *Many Stars and More String Games.* New York: William Morrow Co., 1985.

———. *Super String Games.* New York: William Morrow Co., 1987.

Lankford, Mary D. *Hopscotch around the World.* New York: William Morrow, 1992.

Page, Linda Garland, and Smith, Hilton eds. *Foxfire Book of Toys and Games.* New York: Dutton, 1985.

Classroom Project 11: Traditional-Game Glossary

Some traditional games, such as jacks, hopscotch, and marbles, have their own special vocabulary. The game of hide-and-seek has a vocabulary not of words but of phrases used by players, such as "Ready or not, here I come" or "Ally ally oxen free!"

Ask students to compile a glossary of words and phrases used by the players of one type of traditional game. Some words in the glossary can be special words not used in everyday language; others may be everyday words used in a special way. Students can collect words for the glossary from each other or from family members and neighbors. *The Great American Marble Book* and *Jump Rope!* include glossaries that students can use as examples.

Resources

Ferretti, Fred. *The Great American Marble Book.* New York: Workman, 1973.

Skolnik, Peter L. *Jump Rope!* New York: Workman, 1974.

Classroom Project 12: Art History, Games History

Acquire a copy of Pieter Breughel the Elder's 1560 painting, *Children's Games*, which portrays in delightful detail 200 or more children playing over 70 games. (It is reproduced in color on pages 226–227 of *The World of Games.*) Have students identify as many of the games being played as they can. Many are played today in nearly the same way and are instantly recognizable, while others will require research, using resources such as those that follow.

Resources

Daiken, Leslie. *Children's Games throughout the Year.* London: Batsford, 1949.

Gomme, Alice Bertha. *The Traditional Games of England, Scotland, and Ireland; with Tunes, Singing-Rhymes, and Methods of Playing According to Variants Extant and Recorded in Different Parts of the Kingdom.* 2 vols. 1894, 1898. Reprint, New York: Dover, 1964.

Eliot, A. "Games Children Play." *Sports Illustrated* 34 (January 11, 1971): 45–51.
    This article is a delightful appreciation of Breughel's painting.

Botermans, Jack, et al., eds. *World of Games: Their Origins and History, How to Play Them and How to Make Them.* New York: Facts on File, 1987.

USING CHILDREN'S TRADITIONAL GAMES IN THE LIBRARY

Programs and special events featuring traditional games can be extremely enjoyable and participatory, and at the same time fulfill libraries' goals of implementing multicultural and intergenerational programs. Many of the preceding classroom projects can be adapted for use in the school or public library. For example, traditional-game bulletin boards can be made interactive. Supply materials that allow library visitors to draw hopscotch diagrams, for example, or make folded paper traditional-game artifacts, then incorporate them into the bulletin board.

An enjoyable way to use traditional games in the library is to make them part of story hours. In our experience, this will often inspire members of the audience to share and teach other, similar games they know.

Here are some suggested games for preschool story hour:

- Snail Hopscotch (Argentina: *El Caracol*). You can simplify this hopscotch by drawing just a few squares and making it okay to jump from square to square on both feet, rather than hopping on one foot. Use this game in conjunction with snail stories.

- Make a Caterpillar (Belgium: *Chenille-assis*). Have the children make one long caterpillar and move around, rather than having a race.

Here are some games for elementary grades and family story hours:

- Cat and Mice (Iran: Who Was It?)

- Pin the Nose on the Oni (Japan: *Fuku Wari*)

- Who Can Fly? (Germany: *Alle Vögel Vliegen*)

- Counting to Ten (Italy: *Morra*). Teach this game, and have audience members play it in pairs.

- Philippines: *Hep*. You will probably want to write out a story in advance rather than having to improvise one.

- Tanzania: Giant's House. Use this pantomime game with stories about giants.

- United Kingdom—Scotland: Albert Adams Ate an Alligator. This creative alphabet game is for older, verbally clever elementary students.

- United States: Twelve Days of Christmas. This memory game was the inspiration for the familiar holiday song.

A MULTICULTURAL GAMES FESTIVAL

The following is a description of a week-long Multicultural Games Festival held at Nimitz Elementary School in Cupertino, California, in March 1992. Nimitz School was the site of one of the school district's Newcomer Centers. The Newcomer Center at Nimitz consisted of four classrooms where non-English speakers studied until they had achieved grade-level competence in spoken and written language. The non-English-speaking population of the school included recent immigrants from several countries, as well as the children of nonimmigrant professionals working for computer companies in the Silicon Valley.

Bob Kaminski was teaching beginning-level students in grades four through six of the Newcomer Center when he accepted responsibility for planning the school's annual week-long Spring Festival. The principal requested a festival theme that would bring the students of the Newcomer Center in closer contact with the school's other students. The theme of traditional games was chosen because games are an international language—students who cannot speak one another's languages are able to understand many of each other's games and enjoy playing together. Also, traditional games are played in nearly all American families; they are not a type of folklore that exists in some immigrant or ethnic groups but not in others.

Planning began three months before the festival. Judy Sierra presented an in-service workshop for teachers on traditional games, in which ideas for classroom discussions and projects were discussed. Bob contacted community cultural and educational groups, seeking adults to give presentations on traditional games in classrooms and youth groups to perform at an assembly. He visited the Saturday language schools that many of the Newcomer Center students attended and was able to recruit parents to teach games. He also contacted the school's community business partner, Apple Computer. Requests for employee participation were printed in the company newsletter and posted on the electronic bulletin board. He also arranged for a camera crew from the local community college's cable-access television station to video-tape the week's events.

Two assemblies were held as part of the festival, one on Monday and one on Friday. At the Monday assembly, Nimitz School parents and students demonstrated traditional games. The parents of some Japanese and Dutch students shared a type of traditional game that Bob and Judy had not anticipated: children's party games that are organized by adults (the equivalent of the American Pin the Tail on the Donkey). Japanese parents demonstrated *Fuku Wari* (see page 94) and New Years' juggling. A parent from the Netherlands organized a relay race she translated as "Potato Poo Poo," which was a runaway success. Each team had a chair at one side of the stage and a bucket at the other. A potato was placed on the chair, and the first racer sat on it, picking it up between his legs. Without using his hands, the player then waddled as quickly as possible to the other end and deposited the potato in the bucket.

Students from Taiwan and Korea demonstrated two variations of shuttlecock kicking, and one of the non-Newcomer students demonstrated a modern commercial version of the same game, Hacky Sack. A young man from Vietnam, who came as part of the video crew, showed the students one of his favorite games, Rice-sack Racing (nearly identical to American potato-sack racing). Volunteers from the audience came onstage to participate in all of these games. Finally, the film *Children's Chants and Games* was shown to reinforce the concept that the same types of games are played in many cultures.

During the week, adult volunteers visited classes. Volunteers who did not speak English were assigned student translators. A teacher's husband taught students to play marbles. The school librarian, who grew up in India, taught a Drop the Handkerchief game from her childhood, and a young woman from the school's community business partner taught a sidewalk game using bottle caps that she had played as a girl in Malaysia. A Japanese girl knew a hand-clapping game sung in Japanese but to the tune of "Yankee Doodle." She taught it to a Dutch friend, and the two of them went to other classrooms to teach it.

Teachers led classroom discussions about games that students play at home with their families. It was important for these teachers to understand how to integrate tactfully discussions of store-bought games and organized sports into a discussion of traditional games. Some children who did not understand the concept of traditional games brought commercial games to show the class or told about their experiences in organized sports. It was important that teachers did not reject what these students were sharing. Instead, the teachers focused on the traditional aspects of these games.

Most families have unique traditions that accompany the playing of any game. The teachers were encouraged to ask questions such as, Does the family have their own name for the game? Does the family change the rules of the game? (for instance, most Monopoly players use some rules that are not official, such as putting fine money into Free Parking). Teachers found that many students' families had created folk versions of baseball, basketball, and football to play with their children. The teachers made a distinction between a traditional game passed on by word of mouth and a nontraditional game played in a traditional way as a family adapts it to their own needs.

Nimitz students were encouraged to contribute games to the *Nimitz School Big Book of Games,* which sat on an easel on the playground. There was a Polaroid camera available for them to take photos of game playing if they wished. After the games festival was over, the book was placed in the library for students to read.

A second assembly, held at the end of the festival, featured visitors who came from nearby schools to share even more games. A group of rope skippers came from a nearby elementary school. They had replaced the traditional chants and rhymes of jump roping with rock music. The 16 members of another school's hand-clapping club also came. Members of the group demonstrated hand claps, while one of them spoke the words into a microphone so that the audience could hear them clearly. The third performing group came from a private academy, and these students demonstrated what they called Boot Dances—rhythmic routines of foot stomping and hand clapping, originated by miners from South Africa, where one of the teachers had studied. The boot dancers rapidly achieved rock-star status, and Nimitz students crowded around them after the assembly. A sixth-grade teacher invited them to her classroom so that her students could learn their routines. The group that had the longest-lasting impact on the students at the Newcomer Center, however, was the least polished—the hand-clappers. Students from the Newcomer Center picked up some of their circle claps, and they could be seen and heard performing these on the playground for the rest of the school year.

City officials, school board members, and adult volunteers also attended the assembly. Afterwards, Nimitz parents treated participants, volunteers, and guests to an international potluck lunch.

The events of this week-long festival were videotaped, and Bob edited the tape into a 45-minute program that aired on the local cable-access channel. A copy was presented to the school district.

At the closing assembly, students were invited to tell what they had learned during the week of traditional games. Nearly all of the regular elementary students voiced their enjoyment of games from other cultures and their delight at realizing the similarity of everyones' games.

Film resource

Children's Chants and Games. 16 mm, 15 min., color. Irwindale, Calif.: Barr Films, 1972.

Bibliography

RESOURCES FOR TEACHERS AND GROUP LEADERS

Bell, Robbie, and Cornelius, Michael. *Board Games 'Round the World: A Resource Book for Mathematical Investigations.* New York: Cambridge University Press, 1988.

This is an outstanding resource for teachers of gifted elementary students as well as junior and senior high school students. The authors use a multicultural mix of traditional board games as the basis for exploring mathematical principles.

Harbin, E.O. *Games of Many Nations.* Nashville: Abingdon, 1954.

A useful resource, but only for a handful of countries. Neither African games nor Native American games are identified by nation.

Hunt, Sarah Ethridge. *Games and Sports the World Around.* 3rd ed. New York: Ronald, 1964.

Try to get this edition, which is the most comprehensive.

ICHPER Book of Worldwide Games and Dances. Washington, D.C.: International Council on Health, Physical Education, and Recreation, 1967.

The games in this collection were contributed by members of the international diplomatic community in the United States.

Lipman, Doug. *Storytelling Games: Creative Activities for Language, Communication, and Composition across the Curriculum.* Phoenix: Oryx Press, 1995.

This excellent book contains detailed instructions for using traditional games with children.

Millen, Nina. *Children's Games from Many Lands.* New York: Friendship, 1943.

The games in this book were contributed by teachers in missionary schools, and the quality of the game descriptions is uneven.

Orlick, Terry. *The Cooperative Sports and Games Book: Challenge without Competition.* New York: Pantheon, 1978.

————. *The Second Cooperative Sports and Games Book.* New York: Pantheon, 1982.

Orlick's books contain a wealth of advice for adults teaching and developing games with children from preschool through adolescence. In addition, the author has included many folk games he collected in Southeast Asia and Australia.

BIBLIOGRAPHIC RESOURCES AND INDEXES

Avedon, Elliott M., and Sutton-Smith, Brian. *The Study of Games.* New York: John Wiley and Sons, 1971.

This book is an excellent, if slightly dated, source of scholarly articles and bibliographies on all aspects of games.

Brewster, Paul G. *American Nonsinging Games.* Norman, Okla.: University of Oklahoma Press, 1953.

This work consists of brief descriptions of children's games collected in the United States, along with detailed comparative notes citing similar games from the United States and other countries. The sources listed in the notes and bibliography may be difficult to locate, and many are in languages other than English.

————, ed. *Children's Games and Rhymes.* 1952. Reprint, New York: Arno, 1976.

Along with a classification and description of children's folk games played in North Carolina, Brewster includes comparative notes giving sources for similar games from other cultures. These sources may be difficult to locate, however, and many are in languages other than English.

Culin, Stuart. *Games of the North American Indians.* 1907. Reprint, New York: Dover, 1975.

This voluminous work contains many good line drawings of traditional artifacts used in playing Native American games.

Pilger, Mary Anne. *Multicultural Projects Index: Things to Make and Do to Celebrate Festivals, Cultures, Holidays around the World.* Englewood, Colo.: Libraries Unlimited, 1992.

This work indexes by country individual games that are found in children's books and educational resource books.

Sebeok, Thomas A., and Brewster, Paul G. *Studies in Cheremis.* Vol. 6: Games. Bloomington, Ind.: Indiana University Press, 1958.

This survey of the folk games of the Mara (Cheremis) people of Russia includes detailed comparative notes on similar games from other cultures, along with bibliographic references. The sources listed in the bibliography may be difficult to locate, however, and many are in languages other than English.

GENERAL SOURCES

The following are bibliographic sources used to compile this book, organized by geographic area.

Games: General

Abrahams, Roger D. *Jump-Rope Rhymes: A Dictionary*. Austin, Tex.: University of Texas Press, 1969.

Abrahams, Roger D., and Rankin, Lois, eds. *Counting-Out Rhymes: A Dictionary*. Austin, Tex.: University of Texas Press, 1980.

Anderson, Wanni Wibalswadi. "Ecological and Sociocultural Determinants in Thai Children's Game-Playing Event." In *The Paradoxes of Play*, ed. John Loy, 167–175. West Point, N.Y.: Leisure Press, 1982.

Arnold, Arnold. *World Book of Children's Games*. New York: World Publishing, 1972.

Avedon, Elliott M., and Sutton-Smith, Brian. *The Study of Games*. New York: John Wiley and Sons, 1971.

Bancroft, Jessie Hubbell. *Games*. Rev. and enl. edition of *Games for the Playground, Home, School and Gymnasium*. 1909. New York: Macmillan, 1937.

Bell, Robbie, and Cornelius, Michael. *Board Games 'Round the World: A Resource Book for Mathematical Investigations*. New York: Cambridge University Press, 1988.

Bell, Robert Charles. *Board and Table Games from Many Civilizations*. 2nd ed. London: Oxford University Press, 1969.

Bett, Henry. *Nursery Rhymes and Tales*. 2nd ed. 1924. Reprint, Detroit: Singing Tree, 1968.

———. *The Games of Children: Their Origin and History*. London: Methuen, 1929.

Blanchard, Kendall, and Cheska, Alyce Taylor. *The Anthropology of Sport: An Introduction*. South Hadley, Mass.: Bergin and Garvey, 1985.

Bolton, Henry Carrington. *The Counting-Out Rhymes of Children: Their Antiquity, Origin, and Wide Distribution, a Study in Folklore*. 1888. Reprint, Detroit: Singing Tree, 1969.

Botermans, Jack, et al., eds. *World of Games: Their Origins and History, How to Play Them and How to Make Them*. New York: Facts on File, 1987.

Brewster, Paul G. "How Many Horns Has the Buck? Prologomena to a Comparative Study." In *The Study of Folklore,* ed. Alan Dundes. Englewood Cliffs, N.J.: Prentice Hall, 1965.

———. "A Roman Game and Its Survival on Four Continents." *Classical Philology* 38 (1943): 134–137.

———. "Some Games from Other Lands." *Southern Folklore Quarterly* 7 (1943): 109–117.

———. "Some Unusual Forms of 'Hopscotch.'" *Southern Folklore Quarterly* 9 (1945): 239–240.

———. "Ten Games from Other Lands." *Western Folklore* 8 (1949): 146–151.

———. "Three Russian Games and Their Western and Other Parallels." *Southern Folklore Quarterly* 23 (1959): 126–131.

Butler, Francelia. *Skipping around the World: The Ritual Nature of Folk Rhymes.* Hamden, Conn.: Library Professional Publications, 1989.

Caillois, Roger. *Man, Play and Games.* New York: Free Press of Glencoe, 1961.

Champlin, John D., and Bostwick, Arthur E. *The Young Folks' Cyclopaedia of Games and Sports.* New York: Henry Holt, 1890.

Children's Chants and Games, 16 mm, 15 min., color. Irwindale, Calif.: Barr Films, 1972.

Cole, Ann, et. al. *Children Are Children Are Children.* Boston: Little, Brown, 1978.

Daiken, Leslie. *Children's Games throughout the Year.* London: Batsford, 1949.

Dundes, Alan, ed. *The Study of Folklore.* Englewood Cliffs, N.J.: Prentice-Hall, 1965.

Eliot, A. "Games Children Play." *Sports Ilustrated* 34 (January 11, 1971): 45–51.

Evans, Patricia. *Rimbles: A Book of Children's Classic Games, Rhymes, Songs and Sayings.* Garden City, N.Y.: Doubleday, 1961.

Funk, Ellen Frances, and Hubbard, Eleanor Mineah. *Playtime 'Round the World.* Chicago: Albert Whitman, 1927.

Goldstein, Kenneth. "Strategy in Counting Out: An Ethnographic Folklore Field Study." In *The Study of Games,* eds. Elliot M. Avedon and Brian Sutton-Smith,167–178. New York: John Wiley and Sons, 1971.

Gryski, Camilla. *Cat's Cradle, Owl's Eyes: A Book of String Games.* New York: William Morrow Co., 1984.

———. *Many Stars and More String Games.* New York: William Morrow Co., 1985.

———. *Super String Games.* New York: William Morrow Co., 1987.

Gullen, F. Doreen. *Traditional Number Rhymes and Games*. London: University of London Press, 1950.

Hall, Katherine Stanley. *Children at Play in Many Lands*. New York: Missionary Education Movement of the United States and Canada, 1912.

Harbin, E.O. *Games of Many Nations*. Nashville: Abingdon, 1954.

Hunt, Sarah Ethridge. *Games and Sports the World Around*. 3rd ed. New York: Ronald, 1964.

Hurston, Zora Neale. *Mules and Men*. Philadelphia: J.B. Lippincott, 1935.

ICHPER Book of Worldwide Games and Dances. Washington, D.C.: International Council on Health, Physical Education, and Recreation, 1967.

Joseph, Joan. *Folk Toys around the World and How to Make Them*. New York: Parents' Magazine Press, 1972.

Jayne, Caroline Furness. *String Figures and How to Make Them: A Study of Cat's Cradle in Many Lands*. 1906. Reprint, New York: Dover, 1962.

Kalter, Joanmarie. *The World's Best String Games*. New York: Sterling, 1989.

Kirchner, Glenn. *Children's Games from around the World*. Dubuque, Iowa: Willam C. Brown, 1991.

Lancy, David F., and Tindall, B. Allan. *The Anthropological Study of Play: Problems and Prospect*. Cornwall, N.Y.: Leisure, 1976.

Lankford, Mary D. *Hopscotch around the World*. New York: William Morrow, 1992.

MacDonald, Margaret Read, ed. *The Folklore of World Holidays*. Detroit: Gale Research, 1992.

Mohr, Merilyn Simonds. *The Games Treasury*. Shelburne, Vt.: Chapters Publishing Ltd., 1993.

Monighan-Nourot, Patricia, et al., eds. *Looking at Children's Play: A Bridge between Theory and Practice*. New York: Teachers College Press, 1987.

Mouledoux, Elizabeth D. "The Development of Play in Childhood: An Application of the Classifications of Piaget and Caillois in Developmental Research." In *Studies in the Anthropology of Play*, ed. Phillips Stevens, Jr.,196–207. West Point, N.Y.: Leisure, 1977.

Murray, Harold James Ruthven. *A History of Board Games Other than Chess*. Oxford: Clarendon,1952.

Oakley, Ruth. *Ball Games*. New York: Marshall Cavendish, 1989.

———. *Board and Card Games*. New York: Marshall Cavendish, 1989.

———. *Chanting Games.* New York: Marshall Cavendish, 1989.

———. *Chasing Games.* New York: Marshall Cavendish, 1989.

———. *Games of Strength and Skill.* New York: Marshall Cavendish, 1989.

———. *Games with Papers and Pencils.* New York: Marshall Cavendish, 1989.

———. *Games with Rope and String.* New York: Marshall Cavendish, 1989.

———. *Games with Sticks, Stones and Shells.* New York: Marshall Cavendish, 1989.

Orlick, Terry. *The Cooperative Sports and Games Book.* New York: Pantheon, 1978.

———. *The Second Cooperative Sports and Games Book.* New York: Pantheon, 1982.

Pick, John Barclay. *The Phoenix Dictionary of Games: Outdoor, Covered Court and Gymnasium Indoor; How to Play 458 Games.* London: Phoenix House, 1952.

Scott, Anne. *The Laughing Baby: Remembering Nursery Rhymes and Reasons.* South Hadley, Mass.: Bergin and Garvey, 1987.

Stevens, Phillips, Jr. "Laying the Groundwork for an Anthropology of Play." In *Studies in the Anthropology of Play*, ed. Phillips Stevens, Jr., 237–249. West Point, N.Y.: Leisure Press, 1977.

Sutton-Smith, Brian, ed. *Children's Game Anthology: Studies in Folklore and Anthropology.* New York: Arno Press, 1976.

———. "Towards an Anthropology of Play." In *Studies in the Anthropology of Play*, edited by Phillips Stevens Jr., 222–232. West Point, N.Y.: Leisure Press, 1977.

———. *The Folkgames of Children.* Austin, Tex.: University of Texas Press, 1972.

Van Hoorn, Judith. "Games That Babies and Mothers Play." In *Looking at Children's Play: A Bridge between Theory and Practice*, ed. Patricia Monighan-Nourot, et al. New York: Teachers College Press, 1987.

Virtanen, Leea. "Children's Lore." *Studia Fennica* 22 (1978). Helsinki: Suomalaisen Kirjallisuuden Seura.

World Association of Girl Guides and Girl Scouts. *World Games and Recipes.* 2nd ed. London: World Association of Girl Guides and Girl Scouts, 1988.

Games: North America

Boardman, Bob. *Red Hot Peppers: The Skookum Book of Jump Rope Games, Rhymes, and Fancy Footwork.* Seattle: Sasquatch, 1993

Brewster, Paul G. *American Nonsinging Games.* Norman, Okla.: University of Oklahoma Press, 1953.

————. *Children's Games and Rhymes.* 1952. Reprint, New York: Arno, 1976.

Bronner, Simon J. *American Children's Folklore.* Little Rock, Ark.: August House, 1988.

Cadilla de Martinez, María. *Juegos y Canciones Infantiles de Puerto Rico.* San Juan, P.R.: Casa Baldrich, 1940.

Ferretti, Fred. *The Great American Marble Book.* New York: Workman, 1973

————. *The Great American Book of Sidewalk, Stoop, Dirt, Curb, and Alley Games.* New York: Workman, 1975.

Fowke, Edith. *Red Rover, Red Rover: Children's Games Played in Canada.* Toronto: Doubleday, 1988.

Page, Linda Garland, and Smith, Hilton, eds. *Foxfire Book of Toys and Games.* New York: Dutton, 1985.

Gallagher, Rachel. *Games in the Street.* New York: Four Winds, 1976.

Garrenton, Valerie. "Children's Games." *North Carolina Folklore Journal* 21 (1973): 27–31.

Jones, Bessie, and Hawes, Bess Lomax. *Step It Down: Games, Plays, Songs, and Stories from the African American Heritage.* New York: Harper and Row, 1972.

Knapp, Mary, and Knapp, Herbert. *One Potato, Two Potato: The Secret Education of American Children.* New York: W.W. Norton, 1976.

Langstaff, John, and Langstaff, Carol. *Shimmy Shimmy Coke-Ca-Pop!: A Collection of City Children's Street Games and Rhymes.* Garden City, N.Y.: Doubleday, 1973.

Milberg, Alan. *Street Games.* New York: McGraw-Hill, 1976.

Newell, William Wells. *Games and Songs of American Children.* 2nd ed., 1903. Reprint, New York: Dover, 1963.

Skolnik, Peter L. *Jump Rope!* New York: Workman, 1974.

Sturmer, Fred, and Seltzer, Adolph. *What Did You Do When You Were a Kid?* New York: St. Martin's, 1973.

Wagenvoord, James. *Hangin' Out: City Kids, City Games.* Philadelphia: Lippincott, 1974.

Games: Central and South America

Alzola, Concepción Teresa. *Folklore del Niño Cubano.* Vol. 2. Santa Clara, Cuba: Universidad Central de las Villas, 1962.

Ardon Mejía, Mario. *Folklore Lúdico Infantil Hondureño.* Tegucigalpa, Honduras: Federación de Desarrollo Juvenil Comunitario, 1986.

Beckwith, Martha Warren. *Jamaica Folk-Lore*. Memoirs of the American Folklore Society 21 (1928). New York: G.E. Stechert and Co.

Cadilla de Martinez, María. *Juegos y Canciones Infantiles de Puerto Rico*. San Juan, P.R.: Casa Baldrich, 1940.

Denis, Lorimer. *Folklore enfantin: Chants et jeux des enfants haïtiens*. Port-au-Prince, Haiti: Bureau d'Ethnologie de la République d'Haïti, 1949.

Folklore y Curriculum un Estudio de las Culturas de Tradición Oral en Venezula Aplicado a la Educación Básica. Caracas, Venezuela: Consejo Nacional de la Cultura, 1983.

Gonzalez Torres, Dionisio M. *Folklore del Paraguay*. Asunción, Paraguay: Editorial Comuneros, 1980.

Henius, Frank. *Songs and Games of the Americas*. New York: Charles Scribner's Sons, 1943.

López Cantos, Ángel. *Juegos, Fiestas y Diversiones en la América Española*. Madrid: Editorial MAPFRE, 1992.

Paredes Candia, Antonio. *Juegos, juguetes y divertimientos del folklore de Bolivia*. La Paz, Bolivia: Ediciones ISLA, 1966.

Pereira Salas, Eugenio. *Juegos y Alegrías Coloniales en Chile*. Santiago, Chile: Zig Zag, 1947.

Villafuerte, Carlos. *Los Juegos en el Folklore de Catamanca*. La Plata, Argentina: Ministero de Educación de la Provincia de Buenos Aires, 1957.

Segovia Baus, Fausto. *Juegos Infantiles del Ecuador*. Quito, Ecuador: Ediciones Fasé, 1983.

Games: Native American

Beauchamp, William Martin. "Iroquois Games." *Journal of American Folklore* 9 (1896): 269–277.

————. *Iroquois Folk Lore, Gathered from the Six Nations of New York*. 1922. Reprint, Port Washington, N.Y.: Ira J. Griedman, 1965.

Conservation Society of York County. *Seneca Indians: Home Life and Culture*. York, Penn.: The Conservation Society of York County, Inc., 1944.

Curtin, Leonora Scott Muse. *By the Prophet of the Earth*. Santa Fe, N. Mex.: San Vicente Foundation, 1949.

Daniel, Z.T. "Kansu: A Sioux Game." *American Anthropologist* 5 (1892): 215–216.

Densmore, Frances. "Choctaw Music." *Annual Report of the Bureau of American Ethnology* 136 (1943):101–188.

Drucker, Philip. "The Northern and Central Nootkan Tribes." *Annual Report of the Bureau of American Ethnology* 144 (1951): 444–452.

Fletcher, Alice C., "Glimpses of Child-Life among the Omaha Indians." *Journal of American Folklore* 1 (1888): 115–123.

Fletcher, Alice C. and La Flesche, Francis. "The Omaha Tribe." *Annual Report of the Bureau of American Ethnology* 27 (1911). Washington, D.C.: Government Printing Office.

———. *Indian Games and Dances with Native Songs.* Boston: C.C. Birchard, 1915.

Foster, George McClelland. *Empire's Children: The People of Tzintzuntzan.* Washington, D.C.: Smithsonian Institution, Institute of Social Anthropology Publication No. 6, 1948.

Hirschfelder, Arlene B., and de Montano, Martha Kreipe. *The Native American Almanc.* New York: Prentice Hall, 1993.

Hoffman, Walter James. "Remarks on Ojibwa Ball Play." *The American Anthropologist* 3 (1890): 133–135.

Howard, James H. *Shawnee! The Ceremonialism of a Native Indian Tribe and Its Cultural Background.* Athens, Ohio: Ohio University Press, 1981.

Kroeber, Alfred L. *The Arapaho.* 1902–1907. Reprint, Lincoln, Neb.: University of Nebraska Press, 1983.

———. "Games of the California Indians." *American Anthropologist* 22 (1920): 272–227.

Lesser, Alexander. *The Pawnee Ghost Dance: A Study of Cultural Change.* New York: Columbia University Press, 1933.

Lowie, Robert Harry. *The Crow Indians.* 1935. Reprint, New York: Holt, Rinehart and Winston, 1956.

Macfarlan, Allan A. *Book of American Indian Games.* New York: Association Press, 1958.

Mandelbaum, David G. *The Plains Cree: An Ethnographic, Historical and Comparative Study.* Regina, Sask.: Canadian Plains Research Center, University of Regina, 1978.

Mathews, John Joseph. *The Osages: Children of the Middle Waters.* Norman, Okla.: University of Oklahoma Press, 1961.

McIlwraith, Thomas Forsyth. *The Bella Coola Indians.* Vol 2. Toronto: University of Toronto Press, 1948.

Merriam, Alan P. "The Hand Game of the Flathead Indians." *Journal of American Folklore* 68 (1955): 313–324.

Mook, M.A. "Walapai Ethnography: Games." *Memoirs of the American Anthropological Association* 42 (1935): 167–173.

Morgan, Lewis Henry. *League of the Ho-De-No Sau-Nee or Iroquois.* Vol. 1. 1851. Reprint, New Haven, Conn.: Human Relations Area Files, 1954.

Nelson, Edward William. "The Eskimo about Bering Strait," *Annual Report of the Bureau of American Ethnology* 18, pt 1 (1899). Washington, D.C.: Government Printing Office.

Opler, Morris Edward. *An Apache Life-Way: The Economic, Social and Religious Institutions of the Chiricahua Indians.* Chicago: University of Chicago Press, 1941.

———. *Childhood and Youth in Jicarilla Apache Society.* Los Angeles: The Southwest Museum, 1946.

Oxendine, Joseph B. *American Indian Sports Heritage.* Champaign, Ill.: Human Kinetics Books, 1988.

Pennington, Campell W. *The Pima Bajo of Central Sonora, Mexico: The Material Culture.* Vol. 1. Salt Lake City: University of Utah Press, 1980.

Piña Chan, Roman. *Games and Sport in Old Mexico.* Leipzig, Germany: Edition Leipzig, 1969.

Ransom, Jay Ellis. "Children's Games among the Aleut." *Journal of American Folklore* 41 (1946): 196–198.

Radin, Paul. *The Winnebago Tribe.* 1923. Reprint, Lincoln: University of Nebraska Press, 1990.

Roth, Walter Edmund. "An Introductory Study of the Arts, Crafts, and Customs of the Guiana Indians. *Annual Report of the Bureau of American Ethnology* 38 (1924). Washington, D.C.: Government Printing Office.

Rowell, Mary K. "Pamunky Indian Games and Amusements." *Journal of American Folklore* 56 (1943): 203–207.

Russell, Frank. *The Pima Indians.* 1908. Reprint, Tucson, Ariz.: University of Arizona Press, 1975.

Sherrow, Victoria. *The Nez Perces: People of the Far West.* Brookfield, Conn.: Millbrook, 1994

Standing Bear, Luther. *My Indian Boyhood by Luther Standing Bear, Who Was the Boy, Ota K' Te (Plenty Kill).* 1931. Reprint, Lincoln, Neb.: University of Nebraska Press, 1988.

Steward, Julian H., ed. *Handbook of South American Indians.* 7 vols. Washington, D.C.: Bureau of American Ethnology, 1946–1959.

Swanton, John Reed. *The Indians of the Southeastern United States.* Washington, D.C.: Bureau of American Ethnology 137 (1946).

———. "Social Organization and Social Usages of the Indians of the Creek Confederacy." *Annual Report of the Bureau of American Ethnology* 42 (1928). Washington, D.C.: Government Printing Office.

———. "Source Material for the Social and Ceremonial Life of the Choctaw Indians." *Annual Report of the Bureau of American Ethnology* 103 (1931). Washington, D.C.: Government Printing Office.

Teit, James. "The Salishan Tribes of Western Plateaus." Edited by Franz Boas. *Annual Report of the Bureau of American Ethnology* 45 (1930). Washington, D.C.: Government Printing Office.

Wallace, Ernest, and Hoebel, E. Adamson. *The Comanches: Lords of the South Plains.* Norman, Okla.: University of Oklahoma Press, 1952.

Wauchope, Robert, ed. *Handbook of Middle American Indians.* 6 vols. Austin, Tex.: University of Texas Press, 1964–76.

Wolfson, Evelyn. *The Teton Sioux: People of the Plains.* Brookfield, Conn.: Millbrook, 1992.

Games: Africa and the Middle East

Bey, Ahmed Sabri. *When I Was a Boy in Turkey.* Boston: Lothrop, Lee and Shepard, 1924.

Brewster, Paul G. "Two Games from Africa." *American Anthropologist* 46 (1944): 268–269.

Camboué, Paul. "Jeux des enfants malagaches." *Anthropos* 6 (1911): 665–683.

Davies, R. "Some Arab Games and Puzzles." *Sudan Notes and Records* 8 (1925): 137–152.

Elwin, Verrier. *The Baiga.* London: J. Murray, 1939.

Gibson, Gordon D., ed. *Ethnography of Southwestern Angola.* Vol. 3. New York: Africana, 1976–1981.

Griaule, Marcel. *Jeux et divertissements abyssins.* Paris: E. Leroux, 1935.

———. *Jeux dogons.* Paris: Institut d'ethnologie, 1938.

Ibn Azzuz, Mohammad. *Folklore Infantil de Gumara El Haila.* Madrid: Instituto de Estudios Africanos, 1959.

Junod, Henri A. *Life of a South African Tribe.* 1912–1913. Reprint, New Hyde Park, N.Y.: University Books, 1962.

Kaleel, Mousa J. *When I Was a Boy in Palestine.* Boston: Lothrop, Lee and Shepard, 1914.

Mirza, Youel B. *When I Was a Boy in Persia.* Boston: Lothrop, Lee and Shepard, 1920.

Russ, Laurence. *Mancala Games.* Algonac, Mich.: Reference Publications, Inc., 1984.

Schwartzman, Helen B., and Barbera, Linda. "Children's Play in Africa and South America: A Review of the Ethnographic Literature." In *The Anthropological Study of Play: Problems and Prospects,* eds. David F. Lancy and B. Allan Tindall, 11–21. Cornwall, N.Y.: Leisure, 1976.

Smith, Edwin, and Dale, Andrew Murray. *The Ila-Speaking Peoples of Northern Rhodesia.* 2 vols. London: Macmillan, 1920.

Van Oudenhoven, Nico A.J. *Common Afghan Street Games.* Lisse, Netherlands: Swets and Zeitlinger, 1979.

Van Zyl, H.J. "Some of the Commonest Games Played by the Sotho People of Northern Transvaal." *Bantu Studies* 8 (1939): 293–305.

Werner, Alice. *The Natives of British Central Africa.* London: Archibald Constable and Company, 1906.

Games: Europe

Brady, Eilís. *All In! All In!: A Selection of Dublin Children's Traditional Street-Games with Rhymes and Music.* Dublin: Comhairle Bhéaloideas Éireann, 1975.

Brewster, Paul G. "Burski and Other Polish Games of Chance and Skill." *Zeitschrift für Ethnologie* 83 (1958): 83–85.

———. "Forfeit Games from Greece and Czechoslovakia." *Hoosier Folklore* 8 (1948): 76–83.

———. "Some Games from Czechoslovakia." *Southern Folklore Quarterly* 21 (1957): 167–170.

———. "Some Games from Southern Europe." *Midwest Folklore* 1 (1951): 109–112.

———. "Some Traditional Games from Roumania." *Journal of American Folklore* 62 (1949): 114–124.

Douglas, Norman. *London Street Games.* 1916. Reprint, London: Chatto and Windus, 1931.

Endrei, Walter, and Zolnay, László. *Fun and Games in Old Europe.* Budapest, Hungary: Corvina, 1986.

Fiske, Willard. *Chess in Iceland and in Literature with Historical Notes on Other Table Games.* Florence, Italy: Florentine Typographical Society, 1905.

Fournier, Edouard. *Histoire des jouets et des jeux d'enfants.* Paris: E. Dentu, 1889.

Gomme, Alice Bertha. *The Traditional Games of England, Scotland, and Ireland; with Tunes, Singing-Rhymes, and Methods of Playing According to Variants Extant and Recorded in Different Parts of the Kingdom.* 2 vols. 1894, 1898. Reprint, New York: Dover, 1964.

Gomme, Alice Bertha, and Scarp, Cecil J. *Children's Singing Games.* London: Novello, 1956–1957.

MacLagan, Robert Craig. *Games and Diversions of Argyleshire.* London: David Nutt, 1901.

Mokrievitch, Vladimir de Bogory. *When I Was a Boy in Russia.* Boston: Lothrop, Lee and Shepard Co., 1916.

Opie, Iona, and Opie, Peter. *I Saw Esau: Traditional Rhymes of Youth.* London: Williams and Norgate, 1947.

———. *The Lore and Language of Schoolchildren.* Oxford: Clarendon, 1952.

———. *The Oxford Dictionary of Nursery Rhymes.* Oxford: Clarendon, 1952.

———. *The People on the Playground.* New York: Oxford University Press, 1993.

———. *Children's Games in Street and Playground.* Oxford: Clarendon, 1969.

———. *The Singing Game.* Oxford: Oxford University Press, 1985.

O'Sullivan, Sean. *Irish Wake Amusements.* Cork, Ireland: Mercier, 1967.

Sebeok, Thomas A., and Brewster, Paul G. *Studies in Cheremis.* Vol. 6: Games. Bloomington, Ind.: Indiana University Press, 1958.

Strutt, Joseph. *Sports and Pastimes of the People of England from the Earliest Period Including the Rural and Domestic Recreations, May Games, Mummeries, Pageants, Processions and Pompous Spectacles.* London: Methuen, 1903.

Games: Asia and the South Pacific

Armstrong, Alan. *Maori Games and Hakas; Instructions, Words, and Actions.* Wellington, New Zealand: A.H. and A.W. Reed, 1964.

Aufenanger, Heinrich. "Children's Games and Entertainments among the Kumngo Tribe in Central New Guinea." *Anthropos* 53 (1958): 575–584.

Ayrton, Matilda Chaplin. *Child Life in Japan, and Japanese Child-Stories.* London: Griffith, Farran, Okeden and Welsh, 1888.

Bartolome, C.C. *Philippine Recreational Games.* Quezon City, the Philippines: Phoenix, 1957.

Best, Elsdon. *Games and Pastimes of the Maori.* Vol. 8. Wellington, New Zealand: Dominion Museum, 1925.

Brewster, Paul. "A Collection of Games from India, with Some Notes on Similar Games in Other Parts of the World." *Zeitschrift für Ethnologie* 80 (1955): 88–102.

Culin, Stewart. *Games of the Orient: Korea, China, Japan.* 1895. Reprint, Rutland, Vt.: Charles E. Tuttle, 1958.

———. "Hawaiian Games." *American Anthropologist* 1 (1899): 201–247.

———. "Philippine Games." *American Anthropologist* 2 (1900): 643–656.

Howard, Dorothy. "Australian Hopscotch." *Western Folklore* 17 (1958): 163–175.

———. "The Game of 'Knucklebones' in Australia." *Western Folklore* 17 (1958): 34–44.

Hummel, Siegbert, and Brewster, Paul G. "Games of the Tibetans." *Folklore Fellows Communications* 187. Helsinki: Suomalainen Tiedeakatemia, 1963.

Landtmann, Gunnar. *The Kiwai Papuans of British New Guinea.* London: Macmillan, 1927.

Newton, John. *Village Games of Papua New Guinea.* Goroka, Papua New Guinea: Goroku Teachers College, 1974.

Parker, Henry. *Ancient Ceylon.* London: Luzac, 1909.

Pukup, Kawena. "Games from My Hawaiian Childhood." *California Folklore Quarterly* 2 (1943): 205–220.

Roy, Satyananda. *When I Was a Boy in India.* Boston: Lothrop, Lee and Shepard, 1924.

Skeat, Walter William. *Malay Magic: An Introduction to the Folklore and Popular Religion of the Malay Peninsula.* London: Macmillan, 1900.

Tolentino, Francisca Reyes, and Ramos, Petrona. *Philippine Folk Dances and Games.* 1927. Reprint, New York: Silver, Burdett, 1935.

Yui, Shufang. *Chinese Children at Play.* London: Methuen, 1939.

Index to Playing Environments

For a general index to terms and names, please see page 221.

General Index

by Linda Webster

Games whose names begin with the non-English articles *el, la, las, les,* and *los* are indexed both by the article and by the word that follows.